Better by the Dozen

12 Blocks, 12 Quilts, Endless Possibilities

Susan Teegarden Dissmore

Martingale®
& COMPANY

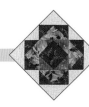

Better by the Dozen:
12 Blocks, 12 Quilts, Endless Possibilities
© 2006 Susan Teegarden Dissmore

That Patchwork Place® is an imprint
of Martingale & Company®.

Martingale & Company
20205 144th Avenue NE
Woodinville, WA 98072-8478 USA
www.martingale-pub.com

Printed in China
11 10 09 08 07   8 7 6 5 4 3 2

Credits

President: Nancy J. Martin
CEO: Daniel J. Martin
COO: Tom Wierzbicki
Publisher: Jane Hamada
Editorial Director: Mary V. Green
Managing Editor: Tina Cook
Technical Editor: Ellen Pahl
Copy Editor: Melissa Bryan
Design Director: Stan Green
Illustrator: Laurel Strand
Cover and Text Designer: Regina Girard
Photographer: Brent Kane

Mission Statement

Dedicated to providing quality products and service to inspire creativity.

Library of Congress Cataloging-in-Publication Data

Dissmore, Susan Teegarden.
  Better by the dozen : 12 blocks, 12 quilts, endless possibilities / Susan Teegarden Dissmore.
     p. cm.
  ISBN 1-56477-628-X
  1. Patchwork—Patterns. 2. Quilting. 3. Patchwork quilts. I. Title.
  TT835.D575 2006
  746.46—dc22

                                        2005033911

Dedication

This book is dedicated to all the faithful quilters who keep this industry alive with curiosity and imagination. Your creative energy keeps us all inspired!

Acknowledgments

Owning a quilt shop in conjunction with writing quiltmaking books leaves little spare time in my life. If it weren't for my hard-working, dedicated staff, I would not be able to create all the quilts that I do. They keep the shop running when I can't. They keep customers motivated and energized, and they provide help on a daily basis that is immeasurable and priceless.

My least favorite task in the quiltmaking process is turning the top into a quilt. Both Eileen Peacher and Sue Gantt are thread artists with their long-arm quilting machines. Willing to adjust their busy schedules to accommodate my book projects, they are appreciated more than words can express.

Thanks again to Martingale & Company for taking a chance with my book projects. I doubt I would be as far as I am without their continued support of my work.

Thanks to Ellen Pahl, my "treasured" editor. She has worked patiently on all four of my books, checking through calculations and providing assistance with just the right word when I couldn't think of one.

Last, but never least, I need to thank my husband, who continues to support my quilting craze.

Contents

INTRODUCTION 6

QUILTMAKING BASICS 8

THE BLOCKS. 17

   CAPITAL T 18

   CHRISTMAS STAR 19

   CORN AND BEANS 20

   CORONATION 21

   CROWN OF THORNS 22

   DUCK AND DUCKLINGS. 23

   GENTLEMAN'S FANCY. 24

   HONEYMOON 25

   SNOWFLAKES. 26

   WEATHERVANE 27

   WINDMILL STAR 28

   YANKEE PUZZLE. 29

THE BLOCK FRAMES 30

    PANDORA'S BOX FRAME 30

    STAR AND CROSS FRAME 32

    ORPHAN ANNIE FRAME 34

THE QUILTS 37

    PANDORA'S BOX 38

    PERENNIAL PATCHWORK 42

    STAR-CROSSED CROWNS 46

    SIMPLY SASHED 50

    JUNGLE FEVER 55

    WOVEN RIBBONS 59

    HORIZONTAL RIBBONS 65

    NO WAY OUT 69

    LIVELY LOGS 74

    ASIAN ELEGANCE 78

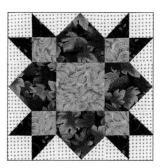

QUILTS USING ORPHAN BLOCKS 85

    FLORAL ELEGANCE TABLE TOPPER 86

    ORPHAN ANNIE 90

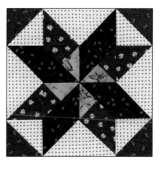

RESOURCES 94

BIBLIOGRAPHY 94

ABOUT THE AUTHOR 95

Introduction

There is something soothing about opening the doors of a closet brimming with colorful fabric, stroking your favorite pieces, and dreaming about the quilt you want to make. *Someday,* you think. *Someday, there'll be time to start a new project.* Slowly you close the doors to your dream, knowing you'll soon be back for another quick peek. Sure enough, it isn't long before you're drawn back to the closet—returning to the fabrics that call to your imagination and curiosity. With each visit, the desire to start a new project grows stronger.

Finally the day has come. The urge to sew is too strong to resist. Even though your busy schedule makes this fleeting moment to stitch feel stolen, you make the decision to start a new quilt. Returning to the closet, you choose your most treasured pieces of cloth. With only a small amount of time to sew, selecting just the right project is crucial. It has to be something that can be stopped midstream and easily started again.

If this sounds familiar, rest assured you're not alone. Like most quilters, I find myself in the position of wanting to use my favorite pieces of cloth but having little time to sew. With inspiration at its peak (and time at a premium), the idea for the perfect project came to me—a block-of-the-month quilt. It's a project that can be done in stages, takes a minimal amount of time monthly, and allows quilters to use the fabric collections that haunt our homes.

With this thought in mind, the search began for 12 traditional blocks (one for each month of the year) that could be placed into a variety of quilt designs through the use of imaginative settings. While searching through my library of block books, I happened upon Uncle Sam's Hourglass. The block featured a Nine Patch center framed with an on-point square and quarter-square triangles. My mind raced with ideas! When the Nine Patch center was proportionally increased and replaced with a different 9" block, I knew I had opened a Pandora's box.

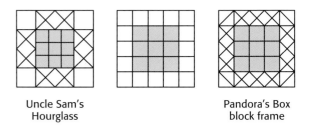

Uncle Sam's Hourglass | | Pandora's Box block frame

The block Uncle Sam's Hourglass, shown at left in the illustration, is increased in size (middle), and then transformed into the Pandora's Box block frame shown at right. The newly created block frame led to the first quilt designed for this book, titled "Pandora's Box." (Directions can be found on page 38.)

The simmering pot of setting designs started to boil faster than I could draw, type, and stitch. In the end, I chose 12 projects to accompany the 12 blocks. Ten of the quilts are lap- to queen-sized, and two of the quilts are spin-off projects that incorporated my "orphan" blocks.

The book is divided into four sections taking you from start to finish in the quest to complete a quilted treasure.

The Blocks. Since you'll need several blocks with a finished size of 9", the first section is devoted to the block patterns. A total of 12 blocks were included in the book, but if the blocks I have chosen don't appeal to you, feel free to choose any 9" block from your favorite source. See "Resources" on page 94 for other block-pattern books.

The Block Frames. This section contains three block frames that were used in multiple projects. The frames act as small borders around any 9" block. The larger framed block can then be repeated multiple times to create a quilt top (see "Star-Crossed Crowns" on page 46) or used individually in a smaller project such as a pillow top or small quilt. The projects using these block frames will refer back to this section.

The Quilts. Ten larger quilt projects that require 12 to 18 blocks each are included in this section. The featured quilts use block frames, sashings, and alternate blocks as setting options. The "Quilt Essentials" box at the start of each project lists the finished size of the quilt, the number of 9" blocks required, and options to sew the quilt as a block-of-the-month.

Quilts Using Orphan Blocks. An "orphan" block is defined as any block that didn't fit well into the final quilt top and was not chosen for that particular project. But why waste them? Included in the final section are two smaller projects using any "orphans" that may have accumulated while stitching blocks for the larger quilts in section three. Of course, you can also choose to make just one or two blocks to create a quick-and-easy smaller project.

So, whether you have just a few moments, several hours, or several days (lucky you!) to sew, let this treasure chest of monthly projects unleash your creative desires.

CREATING A MONTHLY TREASURE

Quilters seem to love the block-of-the-month concept. It allows them to work on a project gradually (as time allows), satisfying both the need to be creative and the need to use up those treasured pieces of fabric we all seem to collect.

The 12 blocks and 12 quilts in this book lend themselves easily to this approach. The 10 larger quilts have 12 to 18 blocks so that you can make 1 or 2 a month. Following the block-of-the-month suggestions at the start of each project, you can easily stitch enough blocks to complete the chosen design in a short 8 to 12 months.

Once your blocks are complete, it's time to think about the final frame—the border. Whether you have chosen a quilt with a pieced border or an unpieced border, now is the time to audition possible fabric choices to find the perfect fit.

If this approach appeals to you, here are some additional hints and tips to help when you are working this way:

- When collecting fabrics for a quilt gradually, consider keeping a record of the pieces you've already used. Glue small fabric swatches of the pieces chosen in previously sewn blocks to index cards. Keep the cards with you when you shop. The swatch cards will help you select other colors and prints in future months.

- Consider saving your scraps in a storage container for later use in the quilt. They can be used in another block, a block frame, or a pieced border.

- If you want the background to be the same in each block, purchase yardage up front, allowing a minimum of ¼ yard for every two blocks you plan to make.

- Consider making a few extra blocks just in case your original color choices don't work. Remember that any orphaned blocks can be used in a smaller project for yourself or as a gift for that special friend.

Quiltmaking Basics

Finding ample time to quilt is truly a treasure for many of us. If you're a beginner, be sure to take time to read through all the quiltmaking basics. I've included everything you'll need to know to make the quilts in this book and have added many treasured tips and tricks I've discovered along the way that will ensure your success.

CHOOSING FABRICS

Once you have decided on a project, the next step is to choose your fabric. Your choice will depend upon the look you wish to achieve. Although I prefer scrappy quilts, several of the projects were made with a more limited palette.

For a scrappy look, first choose a color palette or fabric type. Then select fabrics that fall within your chosen palette or theme. Consider choosing fat quarters (or fat eighths if you can find them), as they are an easy way to collect lots of smaller pieces. While collecting, look for both prints and tone-on-tones that provide a nice variety of color, scale, and value.

If you prefer quilts with a more cohesive look, select one main piece of multicolored fabric first. From there, choose coordinating colors that flow well with the main piece. In choosing fabrics for the quilt "Jungle Fever" on page 55, I started with a multicolored whimsical jungle print. With the main fabric in hand, I was able to select other colors and patterns that worked well with the main piece. The hot pink in the outer border gave this quilt a spark.

When collecting fabric for a quilt with a limited palette, purchase the larger cuts of fabric at the beginning of your project. If you need to add fabric later, it is easier to substitute the smaller pieces used in the blocks. The materials list for each project tells you how much fabric you'll need.

CONVERTING FAT QUARTERS TO YARDAGE

What if the quilt you choose is scrappy but you want to base it on just one piece of fabric? With a little bit of calculation, you can easily convert fat-quarter yardage into a larger cut (or vice versa).

To convert fat quarters into yardage, multiply the total number of fat quarters by .25 to determine the total amount of yardage required.

For example, 14 fat quarters would convert to 3½ yards. Add more yardage if desired.

To convert yardage into fat quarters, divide the total yardage by .25 to determine the minimum number of fat quarters needed. Add more if desired.

Some of the projects list fat eighths as yardage. In this case, use .125 instead of .25 in the formulas above.

PREPARING YOUR FABRICS

I prewash all fabrics prior to their use. Fabrics will shrink at different rates and sometimes lose color. By prewashing, you may prevent a disaster later on. Wash your fabrics on the gentle cycle with like colors and remove them from the dryer while they are still damp. Press them immediately to remove wrinkles. If desired, add a spray sizing or starch when you press to add back the body and crispness that was lost during the washing process. The sizing or starch will make it easier to control your fabrics while cutting, sewing, and pressing seams.

TOOLS AND SUPPLIES

Read the sections that follow for information on the basic supplies needed to make the quilts in this book.

Sewing Machine

A fancy sewing machine is not necessary for general quiltmaking, but a machine that is in top-notch working order is essential. Treat your machine like your best friend. After every project, remove any lint that may have accumulated and change the needle. To keep your machine in good working order, have it serviced periodically by a trained professional.

The stitch quality on your machine is also important. You want your stitch to be even on both sides of the fabric—not too tight or too loose. A tight tension may cause puckering; a loose tension will cause your stitch to come apart.

Rotary-Cutting Tools

Rotary Cutter. A sharp rotary cutter has become a necessary tool for quiltmaking. With care, your rotary blade should last quite a while before requiring replacement. Just be careful not to nick the blade by cutting over pins or your ruler. When not in use, keep the blade closed. It is extremely sharp and dangerous.

Rulers. The acrylic All-in-One Ruler™ from Martingale & Company quickly became my ruler of choice when cutting pieces for the blocks. As well as being fat-quarter friendly, it is handy for trimming the points from triangles when piecing some of the blocks.

Other acrylic rulers that you should own include a 6" x 24" size with ⅛" markings for cutting strips, and several square rulers for cutting squares and trimming the finished blocks. My favorite square sizes include a 6½", 9½", 12½", and 15½". If you need to purchase square rulers and are on a limited budget, start with the larger ones first.

Rotary-Cutting Mat. In addition to the rotary cutter and acrylic rulers, you'll need a self-healing mat made specifically for use with a rotary cutter. At a minimum, the mat should measure 18" x 24". Be sure to store your mat in a cool space where it can be kept flat. Heat will warp a mat, and once that happens, it cannot be reshaped.

Thread

Use high-quality, long-staple cotton thread when stitching quilts. If the thread looks fuzzy on the spool, it is a sign of a short-staple thread that should be avoided. Light gray, beige, or white thread colors will work for piecing most quilt tops. For machine quilting, choose a thread color that coordinates with the top and backing fabric.

Other Basic Sewing Supplies

You'll also need basic sewing supplies, including:

- Scissors for cutting thread
- Seam ripper for "un-sewing"
- Straight pins (I prefer sharp, glass-head straight pins as the head is easy to grab and won't melt if touched by an iron.)
- Basic sewing machine needles (The 80/12 universal machine needles work well for piecing. If machine quilting, purchase needles specifically for that purpose.)

CUTTING YOUR FABRIC

Before you begin to cut pieces for your quilt, the edges of the fabric will need to be straightened.

1. Fold your fabric in half from selvage to selvage (or selvage to the cut edge if using a fat quarter or fat eighth). Keeping the edges together, hold your fabric out in front of you, letting it hang freely. Move the edges until the fabric hangs wrinkle-free. Carefully lay the folded fabric on your mat with the folded edge toward you.

2. Line up a square ruler along the folded edge, and place a 6" x 24" ruler to the left of the square ruler, keeping the ruler edges together. Remove the square ruler and cut away a small portion of the left side of the fabric. (If you are left-handed, reverse this process.) You now have a clean, straight edge from which to cut strips.

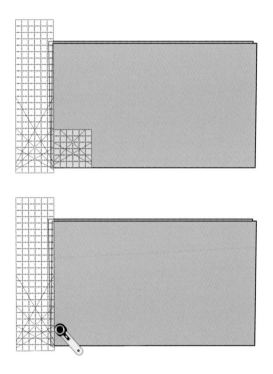

3. To cut strips, move the 6" x 24" ruler to the right, matching the ruler line for the desired width to the freshly cut edge. Cut a strip. Repeat until you have the desired number of strips.

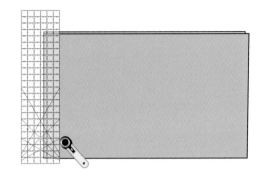

4. To cut squares from the strips, straighten one end of the strip first. Align the left side (or right side if left-handed) of the strip with the desired line on the ruler. This measurement should match the strip width. Cut the desired number of squares from the strips.

Cut squares from a strip.

5. The squares can then be left intact, cut diagonally once, or cut diagonally twice, as needed.

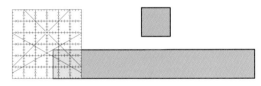

Square cut once on the diagonal

Square cut twice on the diagonal

6. To cut rectangles from strips, cut the strip width to the shorter dimension of the desired rectangle. For instance, if you need rectangles that measure 2½" x 4½", cut a 2½"-wide strip, and then cut the strip into 4½"-long segments.

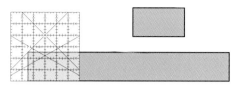

Cut rectangles from a strip.

MACHINE PIECING

Your sewing workstation should include a comfortable and supportive chair with an iron and pressing surface nearby.

Maintaining the ¼" Seam Allowance

All the cutting directions in this book include a ¼" seam allowance. To achieve the best results, maintain a straight, scant ¼" seam throughout the project. Every aspect of your quilt top will be affected if you do not maintain a consistent seam allowance.

What is a straight, scant ¼" seam? A scant seam is one that is at least one to two threads smaller than an actual ¼". This allows for the space that is taken up by the thread and fabric when you press the seam to one side. To keep it straight, I highly recommend the use of a ¼" machine presser foot. If you do not have a foot available, use an adhesive product (such as ¼" masking tape) that can be attached to the bed of your machine. Do not place adhesives on the feed dogs. Once you have attached the foot or adhesive guide, check for accuracy by holding a ruler next to the raw edge of your fabric. The thread should be just inside the ¼" line of your ruler. Adjust the position of your needle or

adhesive guide until you have achieved the desired seam width.

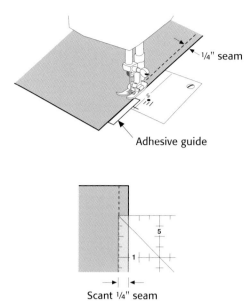

¼" seam

Adhesive guide

Scant ¼" seam

Pressing

Pressing after sewing each seam helps ensure the accuracy of your piecing. Although pressing directions have been included with each project, the rule of thumb is to press seams to one side, usually toward the darker fabric. Sometimes, seams need to be pressed open to eliminate bulk.

Use a hot, dry iron set for cotton. A shot of steam can be used, but be aware that it can cause your fabric to stretch. As you press, use an up-and-down movement.

Finally, think ahead so that you'll have opposing seams within the blocks and rows of your quilt top. This results in seams that butt up against each other, allowing you to match seam intersections perfectly.

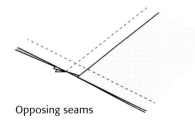

Opposing seams

Chain Piecing

Chain piecing is a process of feeding layered pairs of triangles, strips, or patch units through your sewing machine one after another. It is fast and efficient, eliminating the need to continually snip threads and thread tails. Once you have finished a chain-pieced set, feed a small piece of scrap fabric through the machine as the last piece. Snip your threads and transfer the separate pieces to your pressing surface.

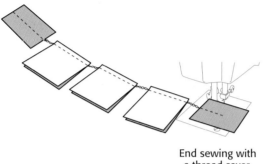

End sewing with
a thread saver.

Sewing Strip Sets

Throughout this book you'll be instructed to sew strip sets. A strip set consists of two or more strips that are sewn together along their long edges. They can then be crosscut and the units can be used alone or sewn to other crosscut units to form blocks or components of blocks.

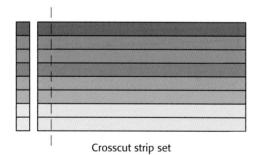

Crosscut strip set

Working with Triangles

Very few quilters like triangles, but they are a necessary evil! Extra care must be taken when sewing triangles because the center cut will be on the bias. Since bias tends to stretch, let your machine's feed dogs do all the work. In this book, you'll find half-square-triangle and quarter-square-triangle units, triangles sewn to squares, and triangles sewn to

triangles to create a larger triangle. Since every block (and thus, every quilt) in this book has triangles, think of it as a skill-enhancing experience.

TRIM THOSE DOG-EARS!

When sewing triangles, always trim the tiny triangles called dog-ears. These little pieces extend beyond the patches after units have been sewn together.

There are a few instances in which I recommend trimming the points of triangles prior to sewing for easier matching. The triangle points make it difficult to know how to line up the pieces, and the feed dogs can pull down the points. Use your rotary cutter and ruler (the All-in-One Ruler is helpful here) to blunt cut the points at a 90° angle, ⅜" from the point as shown. *Do not skip these steps!*

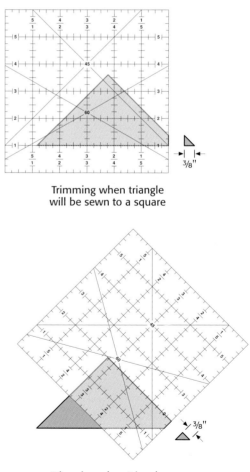

Trimming when triangle
will be sewn to a square

Trimming when triangle
will be sewn to a triangle

SQUARING UP BLOCKS

When stitching components of blocks, I press and trim as I go. If a block is made up of half-square triangles, for instance, I will press the seam and trim the half-square triangle to the desired unfinished size, even if I am trimming just a few threads. That way, when it is sewn into the finished block, it is nearly perfect.

After stitching all the patches of your quilt blocks together, press and trim again if needed. Use a large square ruler to measure them and make sure they are the desired size plus a ¼" seam allowance on each edge. For example, if you are making 9" blocks, they should all measure 9½" before you sew them together. Be consistent with this step, making sure that all your blocks are the same measurement. If your blocks are not the required size, you'll need to adjust all other components of the quilt accordingly.

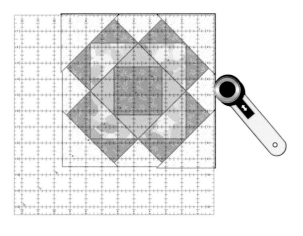

■ ■ ■

TREASURED TIP

Measurements are provided throughout the assembly directions. Compare your pieces to the measurements given and make corrections before you proceed to the next step.

SETTING BLOCKS TOGETHER

Blocks are typically arranged in rows before being sewn together. Pin the blocks together at intersections to ensure that your seams line up properly. Stitch the blocks together row by row and press all the seams in one direction. Press seams in opposite directions from row to row for easier matching. Stitch the rows together.

ADDING BORDERS

When you are ready to attach borders to the quilt top, place them right sides together and pin. Once pinned, you can determine whether any of the seams in a pieced border need to be re-pressed or if any seam allowance adjustments are necessary.

If the quilt top is slightly larger than the border strip (or vice versa), ease the quilt to match the length of the border strip when stitching. To do this, place the quilt top on the bed of your machine, with the wrong side of the border strip facing you.

This allows the feed dogs to do their job; they will move the lower layer along at a slightly faster speed than the top layer. Always handle border strips carefully to avoid stretching. Remove pins as you sew. Do not sew over them as they will nick and dull the machine needle.

QUILTING YOUR QUILT

At this point you need to decide on a quilting pattern and how to mark the quilting designs on your quilt top. Although marking is not necessary for stitching in the ditch and some free-motion quilting, a complex design may need to be marked on the quilt top before it is layered with batting and backing.

Using 42"-wide fabric, most quilts in this book will require a pieced backing. Prewash and remove all selvage edges from your backing fabric before you sew the pieces together. The backing and batting should be 2" to 4" larger all around each edge of the finished quilt top.

Assembling the Quilt Sandwich

The next step is to make the quilt sandwich, consisting of the backing, batting, and quilt top. Your batting choice will hinge on whether you choose to machine or hand quilt. Consult with your local quilt shop to determine the perfect batting for your project.

1. Lay the backing fabric, wrong side up, on a smooth, clean surface. Keep the backing fabric taut and wrinkle-free but not stretched. Secure the backing to the surface with masking tape or binder clips.

2. Lay the batting over the backing. Starting from the center, smooth out the batting until there are no wrinkles.

3. Lay the quilt top, right side up, over the batting. Starting from the center, smooth out the quilt top over the batting. Pin or hand-baste the layers together. Since I machine quilt, I use #1 safety pins for basting large quilts and basting spray for small quilts. Begin pinning in the center of the quilt and work toward the outer edges. Placement of pins will depend on the type of machine quilting you plan to do, but place them no more than 3" apart.

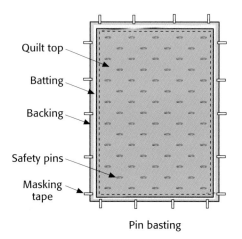

Pin basting

4. If you plan to hand quilt, thread basting is a better choice. Sew a large grid of stitches using a cotton thread. Begin in the center of the quilt and stitch about 4" to 6" apart in all directions. Make the final stitches around the outer edges of the quilt.

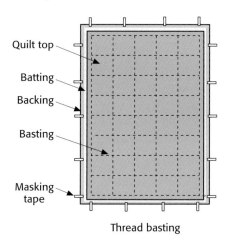

Thread basting

5. Machine or hand quilt as desired.

BINDING AND FINISHING

Binding is the final step in completing your quilt. I cut binding strips on the crosswise grain, 2½" x 42", to make a ½"-wide finished binding. For a narrower binding, cut narrower strips.

Binding

1. Cut enough strips to go around the edges of your quilt, with an extra 12" for turning corners and joining ends. Sew the strips together with diagonal seams, forming one continuous strip. Press the seams open to minimize bulk.

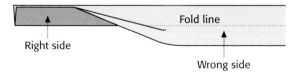

2. Press the binding strip in half lengthwise with the wrong sides together.

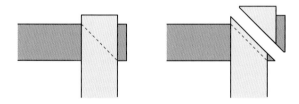

3. Position the binding all the way around the quilt, making sure that none of the seams falls at a corner of the quilt.

4. Leaving an 8" to 10" tail at the beginning, sew the binding to the quilt top with a ¼" seam allowance. Use a walking foot or dual feed mechanism to help feed all the layers through the machine evenly.

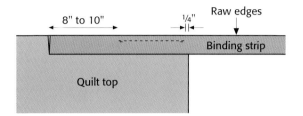

5. When you approach a corner, stop ¼" away from it. Backstitch and remove the quilt from the machine. Turn the quilt so that you'll be stitching down the next side. Fold the binding up at a 45° angle, so that it is parallel to the side of the quilt. Then fold the strip back down so that the fold is parallel to the top edge of the quilt and the raw edges are aligned with the side edge of the quilt. Begin sewing from the top with a ¼" seam allowance.

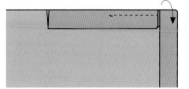

6. Continue in this manner around the quilt, stopping 8" to 10" from where you began stitching. Backstitch and remove the quilt from the machine. Trim the binding so that the beginning and ending tails overlap by 2½". (The overlap should equal the width that you cut your binding strips.)

7. Open and place the strips, right sides together, at right angles. Stitch on the diagonal and trim away the excess fabric. Press the seam open. Refold the binding and finish sewing it to the quilt.

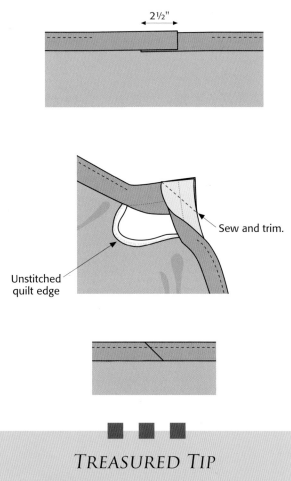

2½"

Sew and trim.

Unstitched quilt edge

TREASURED TIP

Press the diagonal line on the binding strip before joining the ends of the strips. That way, you have a guideline to follow when stitching.

8. Fold the binding around from the front of the quilt to the back and pin it in place if desired. Using a thread that matches the binding, whipstitch the folded edge to the back of the quilt. Be careful that your stitches do not go through to the front of the quilt. As you approach a corner, pull the binding out. With your thumbnail in the corner, fold over the unstitched binding edge, creating a miter. Secure it with stitches. Repeat for the remaining corners.

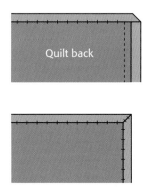

Quilt back

Adding a Label

This step only takes a few minutes and is well worth the effort. Adding a label will document information about your quilt. The label can be elaborate or plain. I like to use preprinted labels, as they are both decorative and easy to use. Using a permanent ink pen, I simply write the name of the quilt, my name, the quilter's name (if applicable), the date it was completed, and the place where it was completed. I fold under the edges of the label and just whipstitch it into place. It's that simple.

The Blocks

CAPITAL T

CHRISTMAS
STAR

CORN
AND BEANS

CORONATION

CROWN
OF THORNS

DUCK AND
DUCKLINGS

GENTLEMAN'S
FANCY

HONEYMOON

SNOWFLAKES

WEATHERVANE

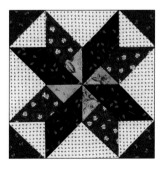

WINDMILL
STAR

YANKEE
PUZZLE

CAPITAL T

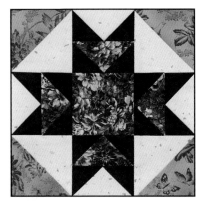

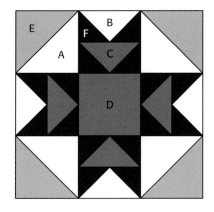

Fabric Value	Pieces for One 9" Block			Cutting for One 9" Block		
	Patch	Shape	Total Shapes	# to Cut	First Cut	Second Cut
Light Print	A		4	2	3⅞" x 3⅞"	
	B		4	1	4¼" x 4¼"	
Medium Print 1	C		4	1	4¼" x 4¼"	
	D		1	1	3½" x 3½"	—
Medium Print 2	E		4	2	3⅞" x 3⅞"	
Dark Print	F		16	8	2⅜" x 2⅜"	

1

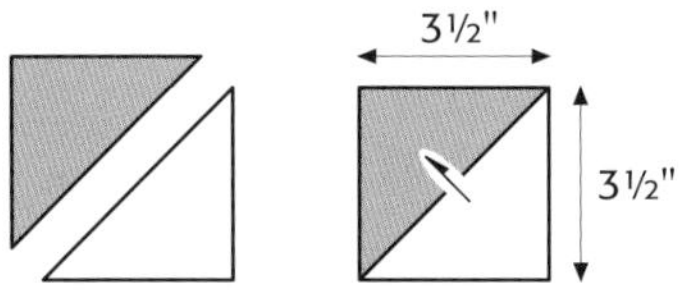

3½"

3½"

Make 4.

2

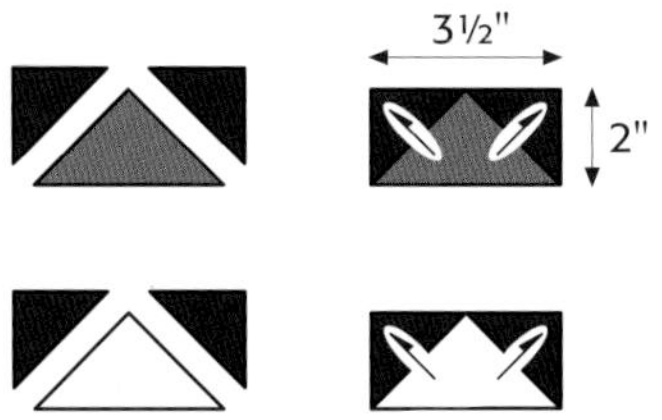

3½"

2"

Make 4 of each.

3

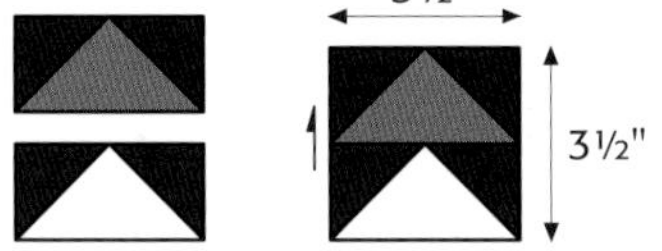

3½"

3½"

Make 4.

4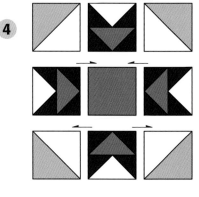

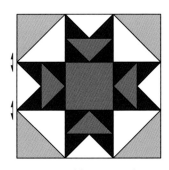

Assemble rows and
complete block.

CHRISTMAS STAR

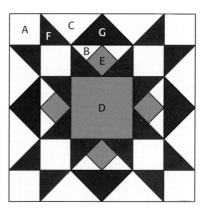

Fabric Value	Pieces for One 9" Block			Cutting for One 9" Block		
	Patch	Shape	Total Shapes	# to Cut	First Cut	Second Cut
Light Print	A	☐	8	8	2" x 2"	—
	B	▽	8	2	2¾" x 2¾"	⊠
	C	▽	8	2	4¼" x 4¼"	⊠
Medium Print	D	▪	1	1	3½" x 3½"	—
	E	▪	4	4	1½" x 1½"	—
Dark Print 1	F	◣	16	8	2⅜" x 2⅜"	�
Dark Print 2	G	▼	4	1	4¼" x 4¼"	⊠

1

Make 4.

2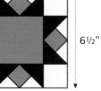

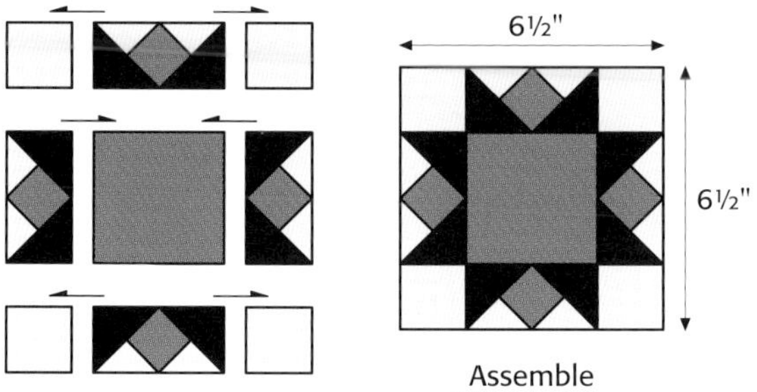

Assemble
block center.

3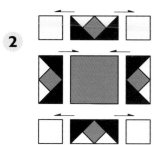

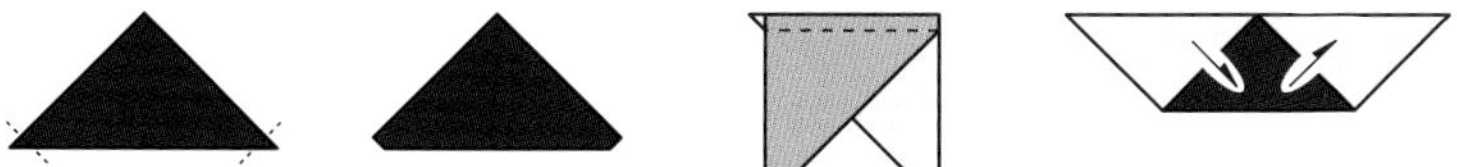

Trim the ends of the triangles.
See page 12.

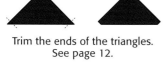 

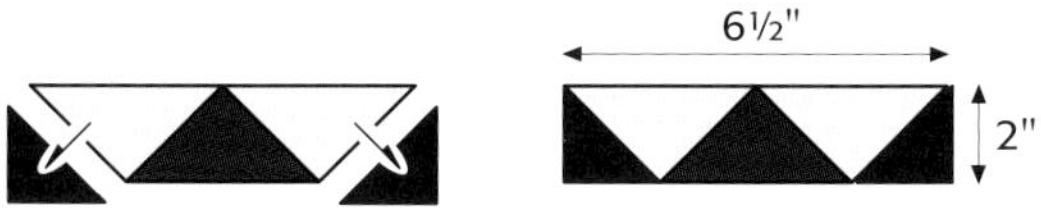

Make 4.

4

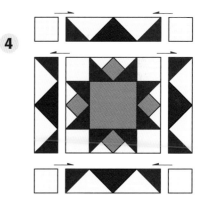

Assemble rows and
complete block.

CORN AND BEANS

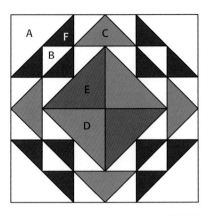

Fabric Value	Pieces for One 9" Block			Cutting for One 9" Block		
	Patch	Shape	Total Shapes	# to Cut	First Cut	Second Cut
Light Print	A		4	2	3⅞" x 3⅞"	
	B		20	10	2⅜" x 2⅜"	
Medium Print 1	C		4	1	4¼" x 4¼"	
	D		2	1	3⅞" x 3⅞"	
Medium Print 2	E		2	1	3⅞" x 3⅞"	
Dark Print	F		12	6	2⅜" x 2⅜"	

1  2" / 2"
Make 4.

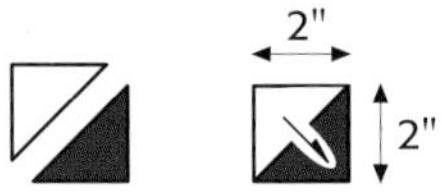

2
Make 4.

3 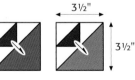 3½" / 3½"
Make 2 of each.

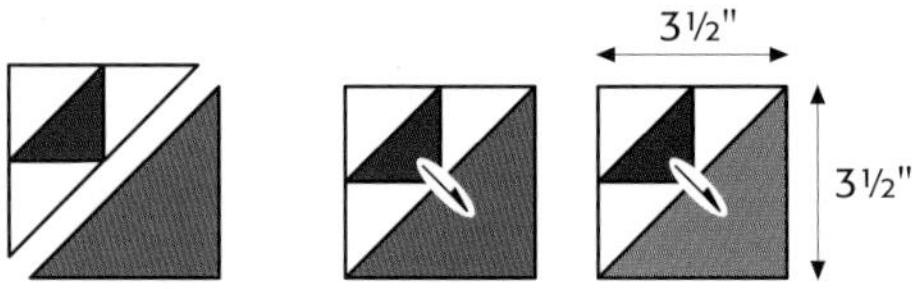

4 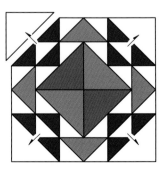 6½" / 6½"
Make 1.

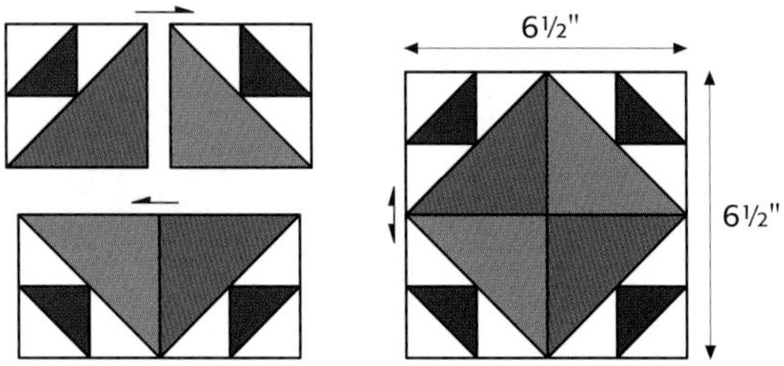

5  3½" / 2"
Make 4.

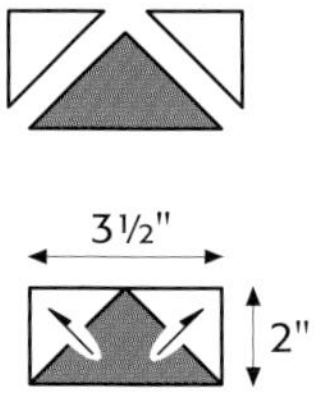

6
Make 4.

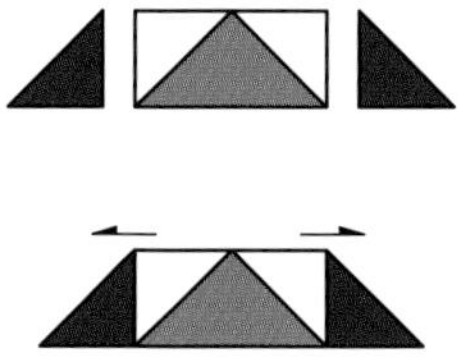

7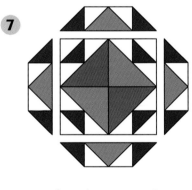

Trim the A triangles before sewing them to the block corners. See page 12.

CORONATION

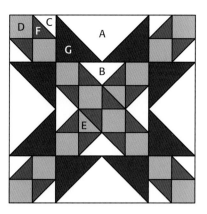

Fabric Value	Pieces for One 9" Block			Cutting for One 9" Block			
	Patch	Shape	Total Shapes	# to Cut	First Cut	Second Cut	
Light Print	A	▽	4	1	5¾" x 5¾"	⊠	
	B	▽	4	1	3½" x 3½"	⊠	
	C	◺	8	4	2" x 2"	◹	
Medium Print	D	▢	14	14	1⅝" x 1⅝"	—	
	E	◣	2	1	2" x 2"	◪	
Dark Print 1	F	◣	18	9	2" x 2"	◩	
Dark Print 2	G	◣	8	4	3⅛" x 3⅛"	◩	

1

Make 2.

Make 8.

2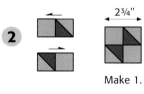

Make 1.

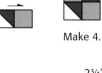

Make 4.

3

Make 4.

4

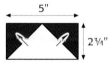

Make 4.

5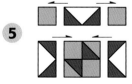

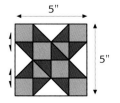

Assemble center section.

6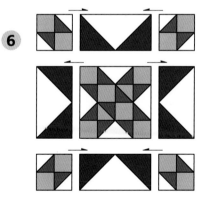

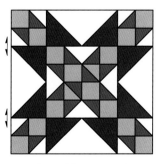

Assemble rows and complete block.

CROWN OF THORNS

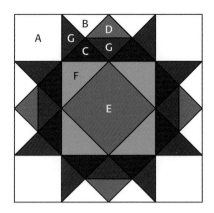

Fabric Value	Pieces for One 9" Block			Cutting for One 9" Block		
	Patch	Shape	Total Shapes	# to Cut	First Cut	Second Cut
Light Print	A	☐	4	4	2¾" x 2¾"	—
	B	▽	8	2	3½" x 3½"	⊠
Medium Print 1	C	▼	8	2	3½" x 3½"	⊠
Medium Print 2	D	▼	4	1	3½" x 3½"	⊠
	E	◼	1	1	3⅝" x 3⅝"	—
Medium Print 3	F	◣	4	2	3⅛" x 3⅛"	◺
Dark Print	G	▼	12	3	3½" x 3½"	⊠

1

Make 1.

2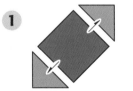

Make 4.

3

Make 4.

4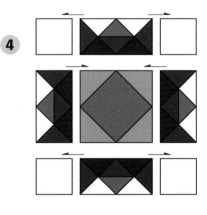

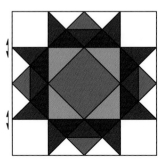

Assemble rows and
complete block.

DUCK AND DUCKLINGS

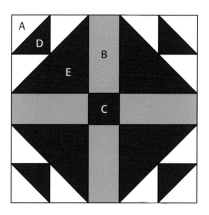

Fabric Value	Pieces for One 9" Block			Cutting for One 9" Block		
	Patch	Shape	Total Shapes	# to Cut	First Cut	Second Cut
Light Print	A		12	6	2¾" x 2¾"	◨
Medium Print	B	▭	4	4	2" x 4¼"	—
Dark Print	C	■	1	1	2" x 2"	—
	D	◣	4	2	2¾" x 2¾"	◪
	E	◣	4	2	4⅝" x 4⅝"	◪

1
2⅜"
2⅜"
Make 4.

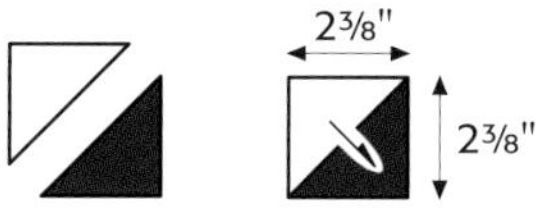

2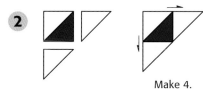
Make 4.

3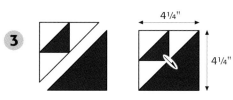
4¼"
4¼"
Make 4.

4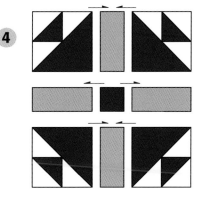

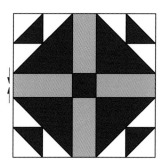
Assemble rows and complete block.

GENTLEMAN'S FANCY

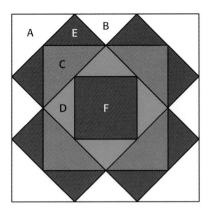

Fabric Value	Pieces for One 9" Block			Cutting for One 9" Block		
	Patch	Shape	Total Shapes	# to Cut	First Cut	Second Cut
Light Print	A	◺	4	2	3⅞" x 3⅞"	◺
	B	▽	4	1	4¼" x 4¼"	⊠
Medium Print 1	C	◣	4	2	3⅞" x 3⅞"	◪
Medium Print 2	D	◺	4	2	3" x 3"	◪
Dark Print	E	◣	8	4	3" x 3"	◪
	F	■	1	1	3½" x 3½"	—

1
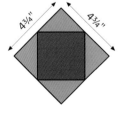
Make 1.

2
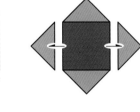
Make 4.

3
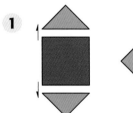
Make 4.

4
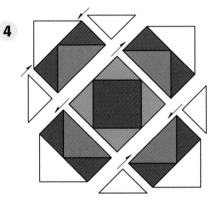

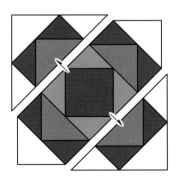
Assemble rows and complete block.

HONEYMOON

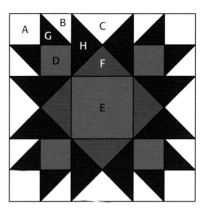

Fabric Value	Pieces for One 9" Block			Cutting for One 9" Block		
	Patch	Shape	Total Shapes	# to Cut	First Cut	Second Cut
Light Print	A	⬜	4	4	2" x 2"	—
	B	◿	8	4	2⅜" x 2⅜"	◨
	C	▽	4	1	4¼" x 4¼"	⊠
Medium Print 1	D	◼	4	4	2" x 2"	—
	E	◼	1	1	3½" x 3½"	—
Medium Print 2	F	▼	4	1	4¼" x 4¼"	⊠
Dark Print	G	◣	8	4	2⅜" x 2⅜"	◩
	H	▼	8	2	4¼" x 4¼"	⊠

1

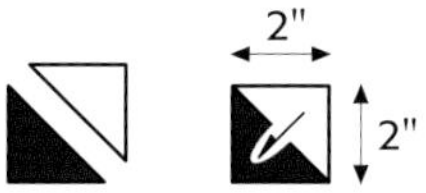

Make 8.

2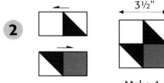

Make 4.

3

Make 4.

4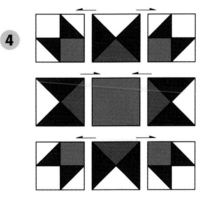

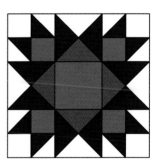

Assemble rows and
complete block.

SNOWFLAKES

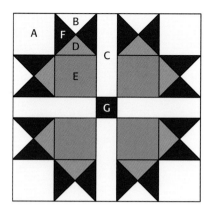

Fabric Value	Pieces for One 9" Block			Cutting for One 9" Block		
	Patch	Shape	Total Shapes	# to Cut	First Cut	Second Cut
Light Print	A	□	4	4	2½" x 2½"	—
	B	▽	8	2	3¼" x 3¼"	⊠
	C	▭	4	4	1½" x 4½"	—
Medium Print 1	D	▼	8	2	3¼" x 3¼"	⊠
Medium Print 2	E	■	4	4	2½" x 2½"	—
Dark Print	F	▼	16	4	3¼" x 3¼"	⊠
	G	■	1	1	1½" x 1½"	—

1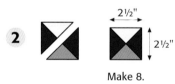

Make 8 of each.

2

2½"

2½"

Make 8.

3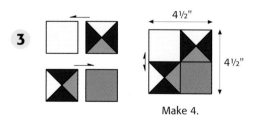

4½"

4½"

Make 4.

4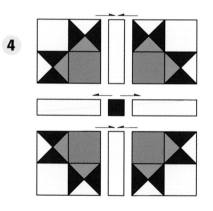

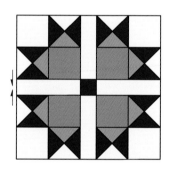

Assemble rows and complete block.

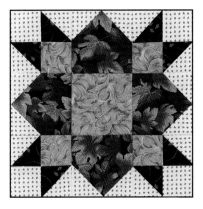

WEATHERVANE

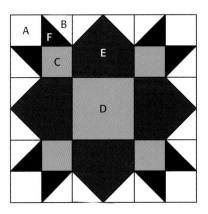

Fabric Value	Pieces for One 9" Block			Cutting for One 9" Block		
	Patch	Shape	Total Shapes	# to Cut	First Cut	Second Cut
Light Print	A	□	12	12	2" x 2"	—
	B	◸	8	4	2⅜" x 2⅜"	◺
Medium Print 1	C	▨	4	4	2" x 2"	—
	D	▨	1	1	3½" x 3½"	—
Medium Print 2	E	■	4	4	3½" x 3½"	—
Dark Print	F	◣	8	4	2⅜" x 2⅜"	◩

1

Make 8.

2

Make 4.

3

Make 4.

4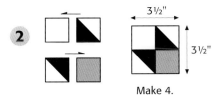

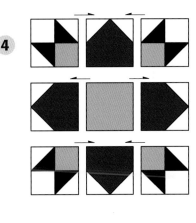

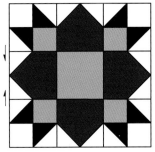

Assemble rows and
complete block.

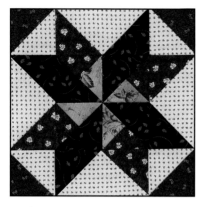

WINDMILL STAR

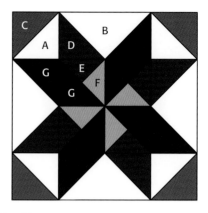

Fabric Value	Pieces for One 9" Block			Cutting for One 9" Block		
	Patch	Shape	Total Shapes	# to Cut	First Cut	Second Cut
Light Print	A	◺	4	2	3⅛" x 3⅛"	◿
	B	▽	4	1	5¾" x 5¾"	⊠
Medium Print 1	C	◣	4	2	3⅛" x 3⅛"	◪
Medium Print 2	D	◤	4	2	3⅛" x 3⅛"	◪
	E	▼	4	1	3½" x 3½"	⊠
Medium Print 3	F	▽	4	1	3½" x 3½"	⊠
Dark Print	G	◢	8	4	3⅛" x 3⅛"	◪

1

Make 4.

2

Make 4.

2¾"
2¾"

3
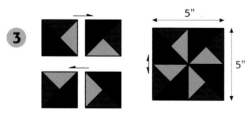

5"
5"

4

5"
2¾"

Make 4.

5

2¾"
2¾"

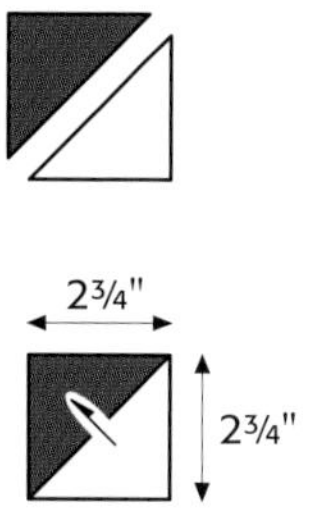

Make 4.

6
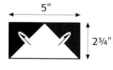

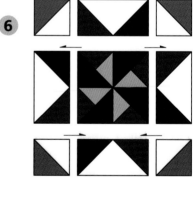

Assemble rows and complete block.

YANKEE PUZZLE

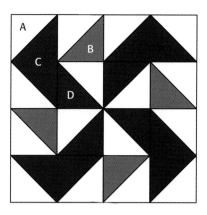

Fabric Value	Pieces for One 9" Block			Cutting for One 9" Block		
	Patch	Shape	Total Shapes	# to Cut	First Cut	Second Cut
Light Print	A	◺	16	8	3⅛" x 3⅛"	◺
Medium Print	B	◣	4	2	3⅛" x 3⅛"	◪
Dark Print	C	▼	4	1	5¾" x 5¾"	✕
	D	◣	4	2	3⅛" x 3⅛"	◪

1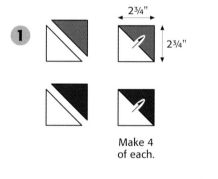

Make 4
of each.

2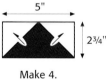

Make 4.

3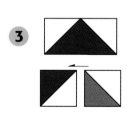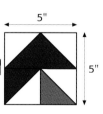

Make 4.

4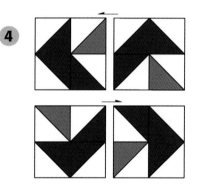

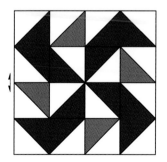

Assemble rows and
complete block.

The Block Frames

PANDORA'S BOX FRAME

Block Frame Rating: Intermediate

Finished size: 15" x 15"

 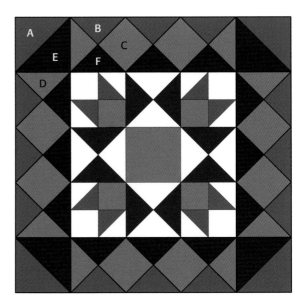

Fabric Value	Frame Pieces			Cutting for One Frame		
	Patch	**Shape**	**Total Shapes**	**# to Cut**	**First Cut**	**Second Cut**
Medium Print★	A	◣	4	2	3⅞" x 3⅞"	◪
	B	▽	12	3	4¼" x 4¼"	✕
Medium-Scale Print★	C	▪	8	8	2⅝" x 2⅝"	—
	D	▽	8	2	4¼" x 4¼"	✕
Dark Print	E	◣	4	2	3⅞" x 3⅞"	◪
	F	▼	12	3	4¼" x 4¼"	✕

★*These pieces can be used interchangeably if desired.*

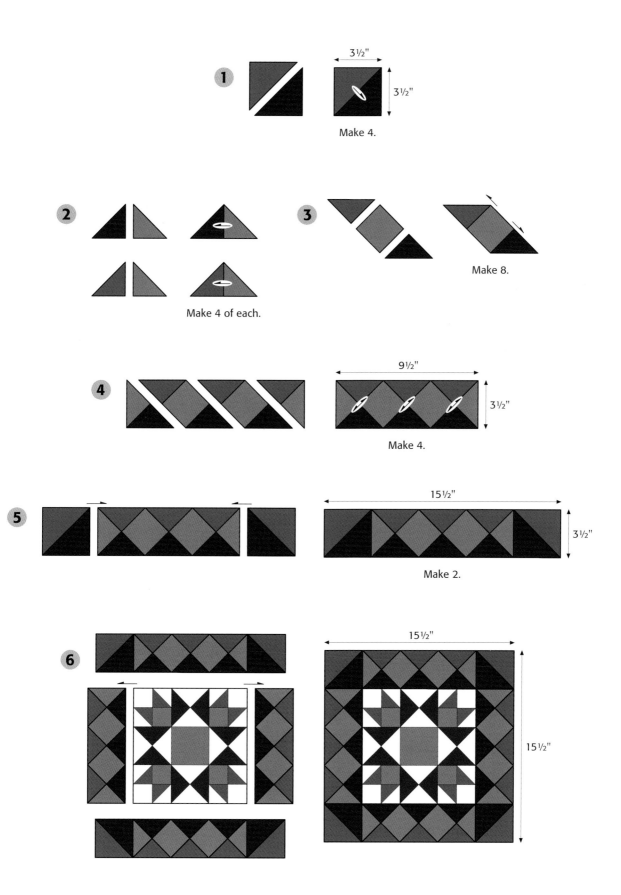

1

3½"

3½"

Make 4.

2

Make 4 of each.

3

Make 8.

4

9½"

3½"

Make 4.

5

15½"

3½"

Make 2.

6

15½"

15½"

STAR AND CROSS FRAME

Block Frame Rating: Intermediate

Finished size: 12¾" x 12¾"

Fabric Value	Frame Pieces			Cutting for One Frame		
	Patch	**Shape**	**Total Shapes**	**# to Cut**	**First Cut**	**Second Cut**
Light Print	A	◺	8	4	3" x 3"	◩
	B	▽	8	2	3⅜" x 3⅜"	⊠
	C	▢	4	4	2⅝" x 2⅝"	—
Medium Print	D	◣	16	8	2⅜" x 2⅜"	◺
Dark Print	E	◣	16	8	2⅜" x 2⅜"	◣

STAR AND CROSS CANDLE MAT

18" x 18"
Designed, sewn, and quilted by Susan Dissmore, 2005.

Stitch a Star and Cross block frame to add to an orphan block. Then add setting triangles to create what I call a "candle mat," a quilted piece used to accent your favorite candlesticks. This could also be backed and made into a pillow. (See "Pandora's Pillow" on page 41.)

1 2"

Make 8.

2

Make 4.

3

Make 4
of each.

4

Make 4 of each.

5

Trim the ends of the triangles.
See page 12.

Make 4.

6

Make 4.

7

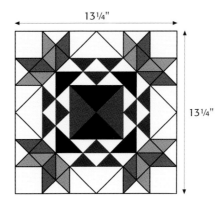

13¼"

13¼"

ORPHAN ANNIE FRAME

Block Frame Rating: Advanced

Finished size: 13¾" x 13¾"

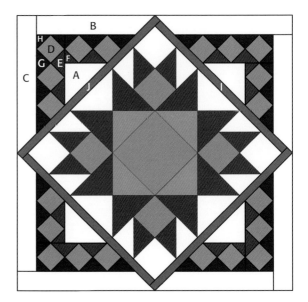

Fabric Value	Frame Pieces			Cutting for One Frame		
	Patch	**Shape**	**Total Shapes**	**# to Cut**	**First Cut**	**Second Cut**
Light Print	A	▽	4	1	4¼" x 4¼"	⊠
	B	▭	4	4	1½" x 7¼"★	—
	C	▭	4	4	1½" x 8½"★	—
Multicolored Print	D	▪	20	20	1½" x 1½"	—
Medium Print	E	▼	12	3	2¾" x 2¾"	⊠
	F	◣	4	2	1¾" x 1¾"★	◪
Dark Print	G	▼	20	5	2¾" x 2¾"	⊠
	H	◣	12	6	1¾" x 1¾"★	◪
Dark Green	I	▬	2	2	1⅛" x 9½"★	—
	J	▬	2	2	1⅛" x 10¾"★	—

★*These pieces are cut larger than necessary for ease of construction and will be trimmed later.*

1. Sew the medium print and dark print triangles cut from the 2¾" squares to the multicolored 1½" squares as shown. Press toward the tri–angles and trim the dog-ears.

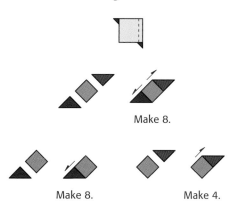

Make 8.

Make 8.   Make 4.

2. Sew the units from step 1 and the remaining triangles cut from the 2¾" squares together as shown. Press seams open.

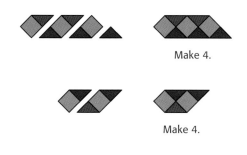

Make 4.

Make 4.

3. Line up the center of the multicolored squares with triangles cut from the 1¾" squares. Sew the triangles to one end as shown. Press toward the triangles.

Make 4.

Make 4.

4. Measure the length of the unit from the very end point to the end of the straight edge. Trim excess fabric and the dog-ears to the measurements shown.

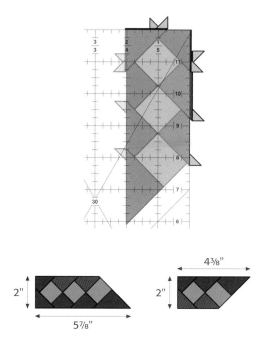

2"   2"

5⅞"   4⅜"

5. Pin and sew the units from step 4 to each side of the light print triangles cut from the 4¼" squares. Place the light print triangles on the bottom, next to the feed dogs, to ease any fullness. Press as shown.

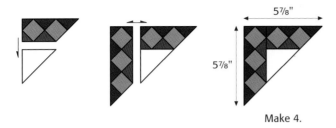

Make 4.

6. Sew the 1½" x 7¼" light print rectangles to the top of the units from step 5. Press toward the rectangles. Sew the 1½" x 8½" light print rectangles to the side. Press toward the rectangles. Place a ruler along the longest edge of each triangle from tip to tip and trim the ends of the rectangles as shown.

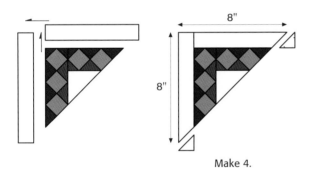

Make 4.

7. Sew the 1⅛" x 9½" strips cut from the dark green to the top and bottom of one 9½" block. Press toward the dark green. Sew the 1⅛" x 10¾" strips to the sides of the block. Press toward the dark green.

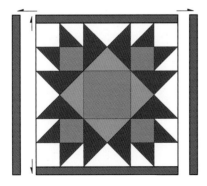

8. Trim each side of the block to 10¼" x 10¼".

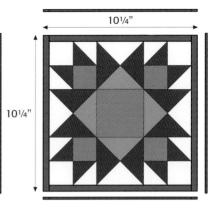

9. Line up the centers of the block from step 8 with the triangles from step 6. Sew the triangles to each side of the block as shown. Press as desired. Square up the block to 14¼" x 14¼".

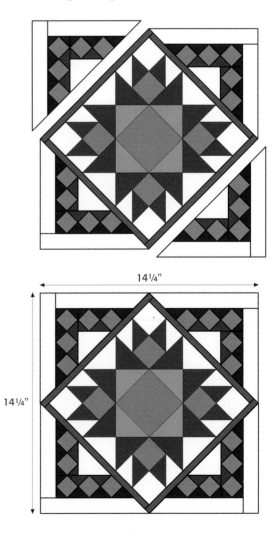

The Quilts

Pandora's Box

Designed and sewn by Susan Dissmore; machine quilted by Eileen Peacher, 2004.

QUILT ESSENTIALS

Finished quilt: 64" x 85"

9" blocks required: 18

Block frame: Pandora's Box

A palette of rich, earthy hues inspired this quilt. The deep colors remind me of a crisp autumn day with cool air and falling leaves that float softly into winter. This is the perfect quilt to use up any collection of fat quarters.

Block-of-the-Month Option

Each month, select one main print (I used leaf and floral prints) and three to four coordinating pieces for one block pattern. Make two each of nine blocks. Using the block scraps, make the corresponding Pandora's Box block frames. When the blocks are complete, audition fabrics for the pieced setting triangles and choose three fabrics that will accentuate the framed blocks.

MATERIALS

Yardages are based on 42"-wide fabric.

13 fat quarters of assorted medium-value prints for blocks and block frames

13 fat quarters of assorted dark-value prints for blocks and block frames

9 fat quarters of assorted light prints for blocks

9 fat quarters of assorted medium-scale prints for blocks and block frames

1½ yards of dark blue print for setting triangles

¾ yard of light blue print for setting triangles

⅝ yard of medium green print for setting triangles

¾ yard of fabric for binding

5¼ yards of fabric for backing

72" x 93" piece of batting

CUTTING

All measurements include ¼" seam allowance. For the blocks, see the cutting directions on pages 18–29. For the Pandora's Box block frame, see page 30.

From the 9 assorted light fat quarters, cut:

- Pieces for a total of 18 blocks

From *each* of the 9 assorted medium-scale print fat quarters, cut:

- Pieces for 2 blocks
- Pieces for 2 frames as follows:
  - 16 squares, 2⅝" x 2⅝" (144 total of patch C)
  - 4 squares, 4¼" x 4¼". Cut the squares diagonally twice to yield 16 triangles (144 total of patch D).

From the assorted medium- and dark-value print fat quarters, cut:

- Pieces for a total of 18 blocks

From *each* of 9 assorted medium-value print fat quarters, cut pieces for 2 frames as follows:

- 4 squares, 3⅞" x 3⅞". Cut the squares diagonally once to yield 8 triangles (72 total of patch A).
- 6 squares, 4¼" x 4¼". Cut the squares diagonally twice to yield 24 triangles (216 total of patch B).

From *each* of 9 assorted dark-value print fat quarters, cut pieces for 2 frames as follows:

- 4 squares, 3⅞" x 3⅞". Cut the squares diagonally once to yield 8 triangles (72 total of patch E).
- 6 squares, 4¼" x 4¼". Cut the squares diagonally twice to yield 24 triangles (216 total of patch F).

From the medium green print, cut:

- 1 strip, 3⅞" x 42"; from it, cut 5 squares, 3⅞" x 3⅞". Cut the squares diagonally once to yield 10 triangles.
- 3 strips, 4¼" x 42"; from them, cut 25 squares, 4¼" x 4¼". Cut the squares diagonally twice to yield 100 triangles.

From the dark blue print, cut:

- 1 strip, 3⅞" x 42"; from it, cut 5 squares, 3⅞" x 3⅞". Cut the squares diagonally once to yield 10 triangles.

- 2 strips, 4¼" x 42"; from them, cut 18 squares, 4¼" x 4¼". Cut the squares diagonally twice to yield 72 triangles.

- 1 strip, 7¼" x 42"; from it, cut 2 squares, 7¼" x 7¼". Cut the squares diagonally once to yield 4 triangles.

- 2 strips, 14" x 42"; from them, cut 3 squares, 14" x 14". Cut the squares diagonally twice to yield 12 triangles (you will have 2 extra).

From the light blue print, cut:

- 6 strips, 2⅝" x 42"; from them cut a total of 76 squares, 2⅝" x 2⅝".

- 1 strip, 4¼" x 42"; from it, cut 5 squares, 4¼" x 4¼". Cut the squares diagonally twice to yield 20 triangles.

ASSEMBLY

1. Make two each of nine blocks, following the assembly directions on pages 18–29. Each block should measure 9½" x 9½".

2. Make a total of 18 Pandora's Box block frames, following the assembly directions on page 31.

3. Sew the frames from step 2 to the blocks from step 1. Press as shown.

Make 18.

4. Sew the medium green and dark blue triangles cut from the 3⅞" squares together to form half-square-triangle units. Make 10. Press toward the dark blue.

Make 10.

5. Using the light blue, medium green, and dark blue triangles cut from the 4¼" squares, sew a medium green triangle to a light blue triangle. Repeat using the dark blue and light blue triangles. Make 10 of each. Press toward the darker fabric.

Make 10.   Make 10.

6. Sew the medium green and dark blue triangles cut from the 4¼" squares to each side of the light blue 2⅝" squares. Make 62. Press toward the darker fabric.

Make 62.

7. Sew the remaining medium green triangles cut from the 4¼" squares to two sides of the remaining light blue 2⅝" squares as shown. Make 14. Press toward the green triangles.

Make 14.

8. Sew units from steps 5, 6, and 7 together as shown to form the setting triangle borders. Press.

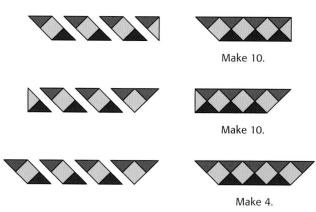

Make 10.

Make 10.

Make 4.

9. Sew the units from steps 4 and 8 to the dark blue triangles cut from the 14" squares to form the side setting triangles. Press.

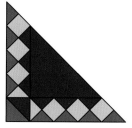

Make 10.

10. Sew the remaining units from step 8 to the dark blue triangles cut from the 7¼" squares to form the corner triangles. Press toward the blue triangles.

Make 4.

11. Sew the framed blocks and setting triangles together into diagonal rows. Press in the opposite direction from row to row.

12. Sew the rows together to form the quilt top. Press.

13. Quilt as desired and bind.

PANDORA'S PILLOW

18" x 18"
Designed and sewn by Susan Dissmore, 2004.

When arranging the final blocks into the "Pandora's Box" quilt on page 38, this block just didn't seem to fit. Rather than waste it, I added an outer border to increase the size to fit an 18" pillow form. I added a backing and inserted the pillow form into the cover.

Perennial Patchwork

Designed and sewn by Susan Dissmore; machine quilted by Eileen Peacher, 2005.

QUILT ESSENTIALS

Finished quilt: 52½" x 66¼"

9" blocks required: 12

Block frame: Orphan Annie

Spring flowers will bloom all year long with colorful floral prints cheerfully sprouting up across these quilt blocks. Watch for thorns, though—this project is intended only for the advanced quilter!

Block-of-the-Month Option

Each month for one year, purchase fat quarters to make one 9" block. Use the photograph as your guide for colors, or select your own theme or palette. When all the blocks are complete, choose one fabric (I chose green) for the Orphan Annie frames (patch F) to accent the other fabrics.

MATERIALS

Yardages are based on 42"-wide fabric.

14 fat quarters of assorted accent prints for blocks, block frames, and outer border

12 fat quarters of assorted beige prints for blocks and block frames

12 fat quarters of assorted floral prints for blocks, block frames, and outer border

12 fat quarters of assorted dark prints for blocks, block frames, and outer border

9 fat quarters of assorted medium prints for blocks, block frames, and outer border

1⅜ yards of dark green for block frame inner border and outer border triangles

⅝ yard of fabric for binding

3½ yards of fabric for backing

61" x 74" piece of batting

CUTTING

All measurements include ¼" seam allowance. For the blocks, see the cutting directions on pages 18–29. For the Orphan Annie block frame, see page 34.

From *each* of the 12 assorted beige fat quarters, cut:

- Pieces for 1 block
- Pieces for 1 block frame (patches A, B, C)

From *each* of the 12 assorted floral fat quarters, cut:

- Pieces for 1 block
- Pieces for 1 block frame (patch D)
- 1 strip, 2½" x 21"

From *each* of the 12 assorted dark print fat quarters, cut:

- Pieces for 1 block
- Pieces for 1 block frame (patches G, H)
- 1 strip, 2½" x 21"

From the 14 assorted accent print fat quarters, cut:

- Pieces for a total of 12 blocks
- Pieces for 3 block frames (patches E, F)

From *each* of 12 assorted accent print fat quarters, cut:

- 1 strip, 2½" x 21"

From the 9 assorted medium print fat quarters, cut:

- Pieces for a total of 12 blocks
- Pieces for 9 block frames (patches E, F)

From the dark green, cut:

- Pieces for 12 block frame inner borders (patches I, J)
- 5 strips, 4⅛" x 42"; from them, cut 39 squares, 4⅛" x 4⅛". Cut the squares diagonally twice to yield 156 triangles.

Assembly

1. Make 12 blocks, following the assembly directions on pages 18–29. Each block should measure 9½" x 9½".

2. Make 12 Orphan Annie block frames, following the assembly directions on page 35. The framed blocks should measure 14¼" x 14¼".

3. Sew the blocks together into rows. Press the seams in the opposite direction from row to row.

4. Sew the rows together to form the quilt top. Press.

5. Arrange the 2½" x 21" strips cut from the floral, accent, and dark prints into 12 sets of 3 strips each. Press 6 of the strip sets in one direction and 6 sets in the opposite direction. Crosscut each strip set into 7 segments, 2½" wide, for a total of 84 (you will have 2 extra).

2½"

Make 12 strip sets.
Cut 7 segments from each strip set.

6. Sew 140 of the dark green triangles cut from 4⅛" squares to the ends of 70 of the segments from step 5. Press in the same manner as described in step 5.

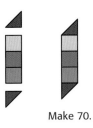

Make 70.

NOTE: For the pieced borders to fit properly, use a seam allowance that is slightly larger than ¼" when sewing the border units together in steps 7, 8, and 9 (after adding the dark green triangles). To check your seam allowance, place the edge of a ruler along the raw edge of your seam. The seam should be at least one thread beyond the ¼" line of the ruler.

7. Using 30 units from step 6, make two border units of 15 segments each. Press the seams in one direction and trim the dog-ears.

Make 2.

8. Use the remaining units from step 6 to make two border units of 20 segments each. Press and trim the dog-ears.

Make 2.

9. Using the remaining segments from step 5 and the remaining dark green triangles, make four corner triangle units as shown. Press seams in one direction and trim the dog-ears.

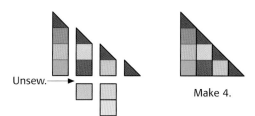

Unsew. ⟶

Make 4.

10. Sew the triangle units from step 9 to one end of each of the border units from steps 7 and 8. Press.

11. Starting and stopping ¼" from each end, sew the border units to each side of the quilt top. Press toward the border units. Align the unstitched corners and pin them together. Sew the seam, beginning at the inside corner and stitching toward the outside corner, removing pins as you come to them. Press the seams open.

12. Quilt as desired and bind.

Star-Crossed Crowns

Designed and sewn by Susan Dissmore; machine quilted by Eileen Peacher, 2004.

QUILT ESSENTIALS

Finished quilt: 54" x 72"

9" blocks required: 12

Block frame: Star and Cross

Twelve blocks are enhanced by green Star and Cross frames. When set on point, they look especially stunning with the addition of a lovely blue floral stripe fabric for the pieced corners and gold fabrics that create a sparkling star as a secondary design.

Block-of-the-Month Option

Choose a white print for the background of the blocks and a large-scale white floral print for selective use throughout the blocks. The medium blues, the reds, and the dark green are used interchangeably as darks or mediums in the blocks. Use dark gold as an occasional medium value. Make one block each month. When the blocks are complete, purchase the greens, golds, floral stripe, and black print fabrics for the final block frames.

MATERIALS

Yardages are based on 42"-wide fabric.

2¾ yards of white print for blocks and block frames

1½ yards of blue floral stripe for block frames★

1 yard of black print for outer triangles

1 yard of dark green for crown points and blocks

½ yard of medium green for crown points

½ yard *each* of 2 medium blue prints for blocks

½ yard *each* of 2 red prints for blocks

½ yard of dark gold for star points and blocks

¼ yard of white floral print for blocks

¼ yard of medium gold for star points

⅝ yard of fabric for binding

3½ yards of fabric for backing

62" x 80" piece of batting

★*If a floral stripe is not available, choose a patterned stripe print. A perfectly straight stripe is not recommended.*

CUTTING

All measurements include ¼" seam allowance. For the blocks, see the cutting directions on pages 18–29. Patch letters refer to the Star and Cross block frames; see page 32.

From the white print, white floral print, dark gold, dark green, reds, and medium blues, cut:

■ Pieces for a total of 12 blocks

From the white print, cut:

■ 2 strips, 5⅜" x 42"; from them, cut 12 squares, 5⅜" x 5⅜". Cut the squares diagonally once to yield 24 triangles.

■ 4 strips, 3" x 42"; from them, cut 48 squares, 3" x 3". Cut the squares diagonally once to yield 96 triangles (patch A).

■ 4 strips, 2⅝" x 42"; from them, cut 48 squares, 2⅝" x 2⅝" (patch C).

■ 3 strips, 3⅜" x 42"; from them, cut 24 squares, 3⅜" x 3⅜". Cut the squares diagonally twice to yield 96 triangles (patch B).

■ 3 strips, 2⅜" x 42"; from them, cut 36 squares, 2⅜" x 2⅜". Cut the squares diagonally once to yield 72 triangles.

From the medium green, cut:

■ 6 strips, 2⅜" x 42"; from them, cut 96 squares, 2⅜" x 2⅜". Cut the squares diagonally once to yield 192 triangles (patch D).

From the dark green, cut:

■ 6 strips, 2⅜" x 42"; from them, cut 96 squares, 2⅜" x 2⅜". Cut the squares diagonally once to yield 192 triangles (patch E).

From the medium gold, cut:

- 2 strips, 2⅜" x 42"; from them, cut 24 squares, 2⅜" x 2⅜". Cut the squares diagonally once to yield 48 triangles.

From the dark gold, cut:

- 2 strips, 2⅜" x 42"; from them, cut 24 squares, 2⅜" x 2⅜". Cut the squares diagonally once to yield 48 triangles.

From 1 medium blue print, cut:

- 2 strips, 2⅜" x 42"; from them, cut 24 squares, 2⅜" x 2⅜". Cut the squares diagonally once to yield 48 triangles.

From the blue floral stripe, selectively cut:

- Several strips, 3⅞" wide; from them, cut 48 triangles using a template (see tip that follows). Cut the strips so that the floral stripe is vertical.

From the black print, cut:

- 3 strips, 9⅞" x 42"; from them, cut 12 squares, 9⅞" x 9⅞". Cut the squares diagonally once to yield 24 triangles.

TREASURED TIP

To aid in selectively cutting the floral stripe, first make a template by cutting a 5½" square from template plastic. Cut the square diagonally once to make two triangles (you will have one extra). Draw a line through the center of the triangle and place it so the line is centered over a stripe. Apply temporary spray adhesive to the back of the template plastic to keep it from slipping when you are cutting. The triangles are cut slightly oversize and will be trimmed later.

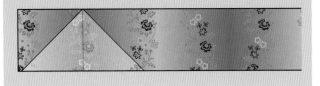

ASSEMBLY

1. Make 1 each of 12 blocks, following the assembly directions on pages 18–29. Each block should measure 9½" x 9½".

2. Make units for 12 Star and Cross frames, following the assembly instructions on page 33.

3. Sew a block frame unit to each side of the blocks from step 1. Press the seams open.

Make 12.

4. Sew the dark gold, medium gold, and white print triangles cut from 2⅜" squares together as shown. Press toward the darker fabric.

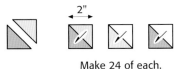

Make 24 of each.

5. Sew the medium blue and white print triangles cut from 2⅜" squares to each side of the dark gold/white print units from step 4. Press toward the triangles.

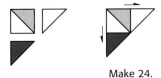

Make 24.

6. Sew the remaining units from step 4 and the remaining medium blue triangles together to form a row. Press in one direction.

Make 24.

7. Sew the units from steps 5 and 6 together to form a larger triangle unit. Press and trim the dog ears.

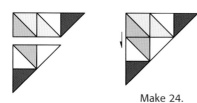

Make 24.

8. Sew the white triangles cut from 5⅜" squares to the triangle units from step 7 to make a square. Press toward the white print triangles and trim the dog-ears.

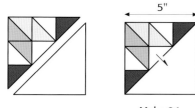

5"

Make 24.

9. Sew the blue floral stripe triangles to each side of the units from step 8 as shown. Press in one direction. Trim the units so there is a ¼" seam allowance beyond the point of the white print triangle.

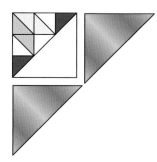

¼"

Make 24.

10. Matching the centers, frame the blocks from step 3 with the units from step 9 and the black print triangles cut from 9⅞" squares. Press.

Make 2.

Make 6.   Make 4.

11. Sew the blocks together into rows. Press seams open.

12. Sew the rows together to form the quilt top. Press seams open.

13. Quilt as desired and bind.

Simply Sashed

Designed and sewn by Susan Dissmore; machine quilted by Eileen Peacher, 2004.

QUILT ESSENTIALS

Finished quilt: 71" x 89"

9" blocks required: 12

This quilt gives the appearance of a midnight sky shining brightly with stars. Simple sashings of hand-dyed fabrics set off the blocks.

Block-of-the-Month Option

Purchase the background prints and gold fat quarters at the start of the project. Then purchase fat quarters of one color group (blue, red, green, or purple) quarterly, using hand-dyed solids and coordinating prints interchangeably for the darks and mediums. Make one block and the corresponding sashings each month over the next three months, repeating each quarter for one year. When you are ready to complete your quilt, purchase the black fabric for the outer border.

MATERIALS

Yardages are based on 42"-wide fabric.

6 fat quarters of assorted light prints for block backgrounds★

5 fat quarters *each* of assorted green, blue, red, and purple hand-dyed solids for blocks, sashings, and borders

4 fat quarters *each* of assorted green, blue, red, and purple prints for blocks, sashings, and borders

4 fat quarters of assorted gold hand-dyed solids for sashings and borders★

2⅝ yards of black solid for borders

¾ yard of fabric for binding

5½ yards of fabric for backing

79" x 97" piece of batting

★*For a less scrappy look, substitute 1½ yards of a light print and 1 yard of gold.*

CUTTING

All measurements include ¼" seam allowance. Consider cutting the sashing pieces from the fat quarters before cutting the blocks. For the blocks, see the cutting directions on pages 18–29.

From the assorted light print fat quarters, cut:

- Pieces for a total of 12 blocks

From the green, blue, red, and purple hand-dyed solid fat quarters, cut:

- Pieces for a total of 12 blocks (3 of each color)

From the green, blue, red, and purple print fat quarters, cut:

- Pieces for a total of 12 blocks

From *each* of 2 green, 2 blue, 2 red, and 2 purple hand-dyed solid fat quarters, cut:

- 1 strip, 9½" x 21"; cut the strip in half to yield 2 rectangles, 9½" x 10½". Reserve 1 rectangle; from the remaining rectangle, cut 3 rectangles, 2¾" x 9½".

From *each* of 2 green, 2 blue, 2 red, and 2 purple print fat quarters, cut:

- 2 rectangles, 2¾" x 10½"

From *each* of 2 green and 2 blue hand-dyed solid fat quarters, cut:

- 1 strip, 14" x 21"; from it, cut 7 rectangles, 2¾" x 14"
- 1 rectangle, 2¾" x 14"

From *each* of 1 red and 1 purple hand-dyed solid fat quarter, cut:

- 1 strip, 14" x 21"; from it, cut 7 rectangles, 2¾" x 14"
- 1 rectangle, 2¾" x 14"

From *each* of 1 different red and 1 different purple hand-dyed solid fat quarter, cut:

- 1 strip, 14" x 21"; from it, cut 7 rectangles, 2¾" x 14".

From *each* of the 4 gold hand-dyed solid fat quarters, cut:

- 5 strips, 2¾" x 21"; from them, cut 31 squares, 2¾" x 2¾" (124 total)
- 1 strip, 3⅛" x 21"; from it, cut 5 squares, 3⅛" x 3⅛". Cut the squares diagonally once to yield 10 triangles (you will have 1 extra of each).

From *each* of 2 green, 2 blue, 2 red, and 2 purple print fat quarters, cut:

- 2 strips, 2¾" x 21"; from them, cut 10 squares, 2¾" x 2¾"

From the black solid, cut:

- 4 strips, 4½" x length of the fabric

From the remainder of the black solid, cut:

- 14 rectangles, 2¾" x 14"
- 4 squares, 2¾" x 2¾"
- 5 squares, 5¾" x 5¾"; cut the squares diagonally twice to yield 20 triangles (you will have 2 extra)

ASSEMBLY

1. Make 12 blocks, following the assembly directions on pages 18–29. Each block should measure 9½" x 9½".

2. Sew the 2¾" x 10½" rectangles cut from two green prints to each side of the 9½" x 10½" green hand-dyed solid rectangles as shown. Press toward the solid green. Cut each strip set into three segments, 2¾" wide. Repeat with the blue, red, and purple fabrics.

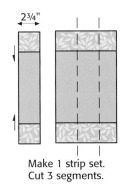

Make 1 strip set.
Cut 3 segments.

3. Sew two different 2¾" x 9½" green rectangles to opposite sides of a green pieced block. Press toward the rectangles. Sew green segments from step 2 to the top and bottom of the block, matching the side fabrics as shown. Press away from the blocks. Repeat with the green, blue, red, and purple fabrics and pieced blocks to make three of each color combination.

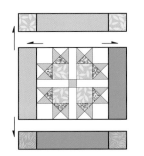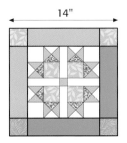

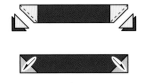

Make 3 of each.

4. With right sides together, place a gold 2¾" square on each end of a 2¾" x 14" green hand-dyed solid rectangle. Draw a diagonal line on each gold square as shown and sew on the line. Trim away the excess fabric, leaving a ¼" seam allowance. Press toward the gold. Repeat to make eight of the same green units.

Make 8.

5. Repeat step 4 with the remaining 2¾" x 14" hand-dyed solid green, blue, red, and purple rectangles to make the combinations and quantities as shown.

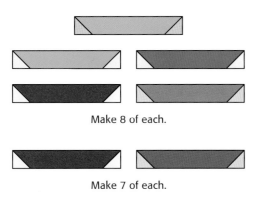

Make 8 of each.

Make 7 of each.

6. Sew a green print 2¾" square to each end of five of the green units from step 4. Press toward the squares.

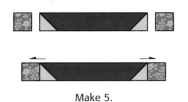

Make 5.

7. Repeat step 6 with units from step 5 and the green, blue, red, and purple print squares in the combinations and quantities shown.

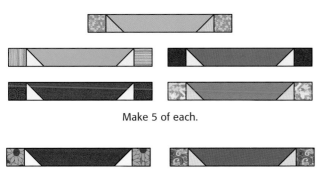

Make 5 of each.

Make 4 of each.

8. Sew the units from steps 3 through 7 together to form a larger block. Press toward the center. Repeat to make 12 blocks as shown above right.

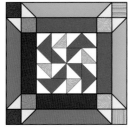

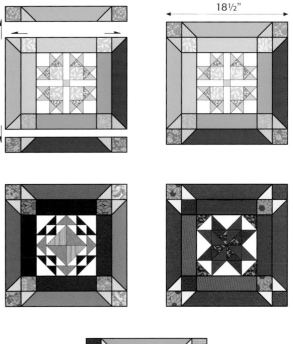

18½"

Make 3 of each.

9. Sew the blocks together into rows. Press in the opposite direction from row to row. Sew the rows together to form the quilt top. Press.

10. Sew the remaining purple and red print squares to the remaining units from step 7 to form the first inner-border strips. Press in the opposite direction that you pressed the quilt top in step 9.

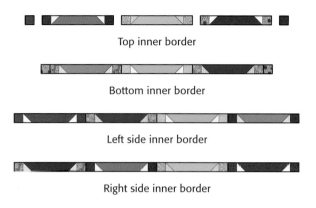

Top inner border

Bottom inner border

Left side inner border

Right side inner border

11. Sew the side inner borders to the quilt top. Press as desired. Sew the top and bottom inner borders to the quilt. Press.

12. Sew the gold triangles cut from 3⅛" squares to each side of the black triangles cut from 5¾" squares. Press toward the gold fabric and trim the dog-ears. The units should measure 2¾" x 5".

Make 18.

13. Sew the units from step 12 to the black 2¾" x 14" rectangles and the black 2¾" squares to form the middle border.

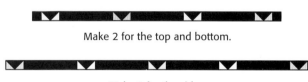

Make 2 for the top and bottom.

Make 2 for the sides.

14. Sew the side borders to the quilt and press as desired. Sew the top and bottom borders to the quilt and press.

15. Measure the quilt from top to bottom and cut two of the 4½"-wide black outer-border strips to that measurement. Sew the strips to the sides of the quilt. Press toward the outer border.

16. Measure the quilt from side to side (including borders just added) and cut the two remaining black outer-border strips to that measurement. Sew the strips to the top and bottom of the quilt. Press toward the outer border.

17. Quilt as desired and bind.

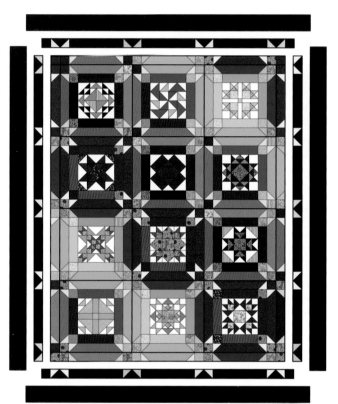

Jungle Fever

Designed and sewn by Susan Dissmore; machine quilted by Eileen Peacher, 2005.

QUILT ESSENTIALS

Finished quilt: 63" x 76½"

9" blocks required: 12

Catch the fever with hot pink, clear blue, lime green, and bright yellow mixed with a whimsical jungle print in this cheerful 12-block sashed quilt. It's easy to change the look of the quilt with another fun theme fabric.

Block-of-the-Month Option

At the beginning of the project, purchase 2½ yards of a white background and ¾ yard of a theme print for use in each of the 12 blocks. Other colors for the blocks can be purchased as needed. Additional green, pink, and blue fabrics for the sashings and outer border can be purchased when you are ready to complete your quilt.

MATERIALS

Yardages are based on 42"-wide fabric.

2½ yards of light background for blocks, sashing, and inner border

2⅛ yards of dark blue for blocks, sashing, and borders

⅞ yard of green plaid for blocks and sashing

⅞ yard of green print for blocks and sashing

¾ yard of jungle theme print for blocks

¾ yard of dark pink for blocks and inner border

¾ yard of medium pink for blocks and inner border

¾ yard of medium blue for blocks, sashing, and inner border

6 fat eighths of assorted contrasting prints for blocks

⅝ yard of fabric for binding

4¾ yards of fabric for backing

71" x 85" piece of batting

CUTTING

All measurements include ¼" seam allowance. Cut the lengthwise border pieces from the dark blue before you cut the blocks. For the blocks, see the cutting directions on pages 18–29.

From all the fabrics for blocks, cut:

- Pieces for a total of 12 blocks

From *each* of the green plaid and green print fabrics, cut:

- 3 strips, 2¾" x 42"
- 2 strips, 5¾" x 42"; from them, cut 8 squares, 5¾" x 5¾". Cut the squares diagonally twice to yield 32 triangles (you will have 1 extra).

From the medium blue, cut:

- 3 to 4 strips, 5¾" x 42"; from them, cut 20 squares, 5¾" x 5¾". Cut the squares diagonally twice to yield 80 triangles.

From the light background, cut:

- 6 to 7 strips, 5¾" x 42"; from them, cut 38 squares, 5¾" x 5¾". Cut the squares diagonally twice to yield 152 triangles.

From *each* of the dark and medium pink fabrics, cut:

- 2 to 3 strips, 5¾" x 42"; from them, cut 14 squares, 5¾" x 5¾". Cut the squares diagonally twice to yield 56 triangles (you will have 2 extra).

From the dark blue, cut:

- 4 strips, 5" x length fabric

From the remaining dark blue, cut:

- 12 squares, 5¾" x 5¾"; cut the squares diagonally twice to yield 48 triangles (you will have 2 extra).

ASSEMBLY

1. Make 12 blocks, following the assembly directions on pages 18–29. Each block should measure 9½" x 9½".

2. Sew the 2¾" x 42" strips of green plaid and green print into pairs to form three strip sets. Press toward the green plaid. Crosscut the strip sets into 40 segments, 2¾" wide.

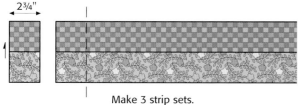

Make 3 strip sets.
Cut 40 segments.

3. Sew the crosscut segments from step 2 together to form the Four Patch blocks. Press.

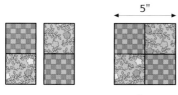

Make 20.

4. Sew the medium blue, green plaid, green print, and light background triangles cut from 5¾" squares together to form larger triangles. Press toward the darker fabric.

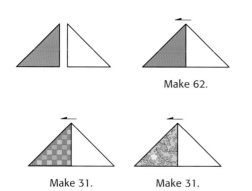

Make 62.

Make 31.   Make 31.

5. Join the triangles from step 4 to form quarter-square blocks. Press and trim the dog-ears.

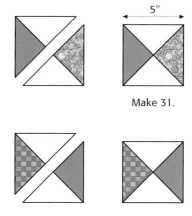

Make 31.

Make 31.

6. Sew the units from step 5 into pairs to form sashing units. Press toward the darker triangle.

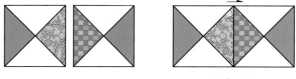

Make 31.

7. Sew the blocks from step 3 and 15 of the units from step 6 together to form the sashing rows. Press. Sew the sashing rows and the remaining sashing units to the blocks as shown. Press.

8. Sew the medium pink, dark pink, dark blue, medium blue, and light background triangles cut from 5¾" squares together to form larger triangles. Press toward the darker fabric.

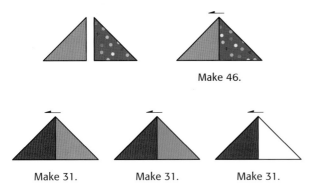

Make 46.

Make 31.   Make 31.   Make 31.

9. Sew the triangles from step 8 together to form quarter-square blocks. Press and trim the dog-ears.

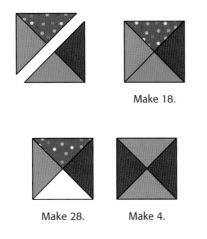

Make 18.

Make 28.   Make 4.

10. Sew the units from step 9 together to form the inner-border units as shown in the quilt diagram. Press in the opposite direction of the quilt top.

11. Sew the side border units to the quilt top. Press. Sew the top and bottom border units to the quilt top. Press.

12. Measure the quilt from top to bottom and cut two of the 5"-wide dark blue outer-border strips to that measurement. Sew the strips to the sides of the quilt. Press toward the outer border.

13. Measure the quilt from side to side (including borders just added) and cut the two remaining dark blue outer-border strips to that measurement. Sew the strips to the top and bottom of the quilt. Press toward the outer border.

14. Quilt as desired and bind.

Woven Ribbons

Designed and sewn by Susan Dissmore; machine quilted by Eileen Peacher, 2004.

QUILT ESSENTIALS

Finished quilt: 88" x 110½"

9" blocks required: 18

Ribbons of gold weave through intertwined shades of green, softly framing 18 richly colored blocks.

Block-of-the-Month Option

At the start of the project, purchase 1¾ yards of a light beige for the block backgrounds. Each month for nine months, select fat eighths for one block pattern. Make two each of any nine blocks. When you are ready to complete the quilt, purchase complementary fabrics for the block frames, sashings, setting triangles, and outer borders.

MATERIALS

Yardages are based on 42"-wide fabric.

4⅝ yards of dark green print for block frames, sashing, setting triangles, and outer border★

2¾ yards of medium green for block frames, sashing, and setting triangles

1¾ yards of beige for blocks

1⅝ yards of light green for block frames and setting triangles

1½ yards of dark gold for block frames, setting triangles, and inner border

1¼ yards of medium gold for block frames and setting triangles

26 fat eighths of assorted medium and dark prints for blocks

⅞ yard of fabric for binding

8¼ yards of fabric for backing

96" x 119" piece of batting

★*2¾ yards are allowed for the outer border.*

CUTTING

All measurements include ¼" seam allowance. For the blocks, see the cutting directions on pages 18–29. Cut the lengthwise border pieces from the dark green print after cutting all the other pieces.

From the beige fabric and assorted medium and dark fat eighths, cut:

- Pieces for a total of 18 blocks

From the medium green, cut:

- 37 strips, 1½" x 42"
- 2 strips, 1½" x 42"; from them, cut 28 squares, 1½" x 1½"
- 2 strips, 15½" x 42"; from them, cut 48 rectangles, 1½" x 15½"

From the light green, cut:

- 33 strips, 1½" x 42"

From the dark green print, cut:

- 11 strips, 1½" x 42"
- 1 strip, 1½" x 42"; from it, cut 17 squares, 1½" x 1½"
- 2 strips, 2⅝" x 42"; from them, cut 25 squares, 2⅝" x 2⅝". Cut the squares diagonally twice to yield 100 triangles (you will have 2 extra).
- 2 strips, 14" x 42"; from them, cut 3 squares, 14" x 14". Cut the squares diagonally twice to yield 12 triangles (you will have 2 extra).
- 2 squares, 7¼" x 7¼"; cut the squares diagonally once to yield 4 triangles
- 4 strips, 9½" x length of fabric

From the dark gold, cut:

- 4 strips, 7½" x 42"
- 10 strips, 1½" x 42"

From the medium gold, cut:

- 4 strips, 9½" x 42"; from them, cut 96 rectangles, 1½" x 9½"

ASSEMBLY

1. Make two each of nine blocks, following the assembly directions on pages 18–29. Each block should measure 9½" x 9½".

2. Sew 20 of the medium green and 16 of the light green 1½"-wide strips together to form four strip sets as shown. Press toward the light green. Crosscut the strip sets into 96 segments, 1½" wide.

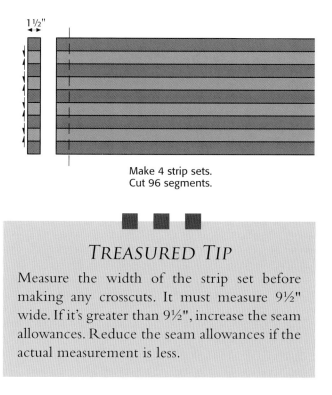

Make 4 strip sets.
Cut 96 segments.

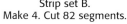

TREASURED TIP

Measure the width of the strip set before making any crosscuts. It must measure 9½" wide. If it's greater than 9½", increase the seam allowances. Reduce the seam allowances if the actual measurement is less.

3. Sew the dark, medium, and light green 1½"-wide strips together into strip sets as shown. Make seven of strip set A and crosscut 164 segments, 1½" wide. Make four of strip set B and crosscut 82 segments, 1½" wide. Press toward the medium green.

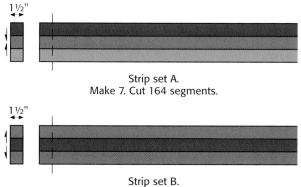

Strip set A.
Make 7. Cut 164 segments.

Strip set B.
Make 4. Cut 82 segments.

4. Sew the crosscut segments from step 3 together to make a total of 82 Nine Patch blocks as shown. Press.

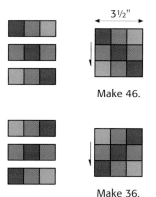

3½"

Make 46.

Make 36.

5. Sew a light green 1½"-wide strip to each side of the dark gold 7½"-wide strips. Press toward the light green. Crosscut the strip sets into 96 segments, 1½" wide.

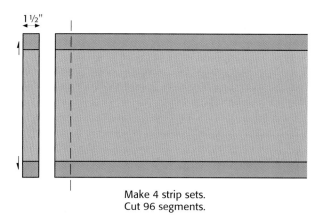

Make 4 strip sets.
Cut 96 segments.

6. Join the units from step 2, step 5, and the medium gold 1½" x 9½" rectangles to form the block frames. Press toward the gold rectangles.

Make 96.

7. Sew 72 of the Nine Patch blocks from step 4 to each side of 36 of the units from step 6. Press.

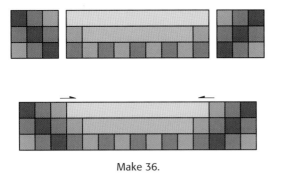

Make 36.

8. Sew 36 of the units from step 6 to opposite sides of the 18 blocks from step 1. Press.

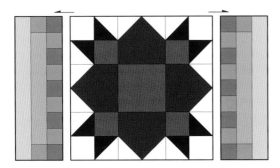

9. Sew the units from step 7 to the remaining sides of the blocks from step 8. Press.

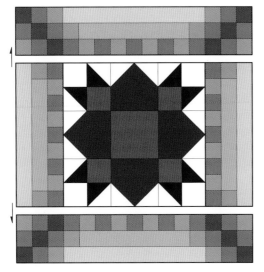

Make 18.

10. Sew the remaining light green 1½"-wide strips and medium green 1½"-wide strips into pairs to make two strip sets. Press toward the medium green. Crosscut the strip sets into 28 segments, 1½" wide.

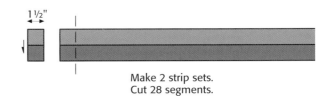

Make 2 strip sets.
Cut 28 segments.

11. Sew 28 of the dark green triangles cut from 2⅝" squares to the end of the units from step 10. Press toward the dark green.

Make 28.

12. Sew 56 of the dark green triangles cut from 2⅝" squares to two adjoining sides of each medium green 1½" square. Press as shown.

Make 28.

13. Sew the units from steps 11 and 12 together to form triangle units.

Make 28.

14. Sew the remaining units from steps 4 and 6 to the units from step 13 as shown. Press.

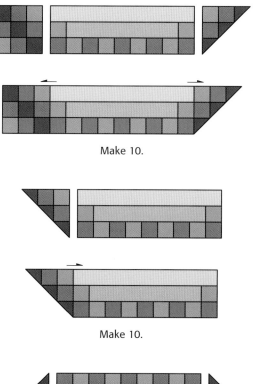

Make 10.

Make 10.

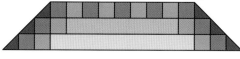

Make 4.

15. Sew the units from step 14 to the 10 dark green triangles cut from 14" squares and the 4 dark green triangles cut from 7¼" squares. Press toward the triangles.

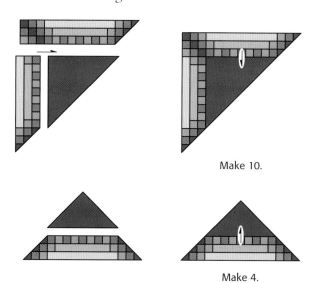

Make 10.

Make 4.

16. Sew the blocks, the medium green 1½" x 15½" sashing pieces, and the setting triangles together into diagonal rows. Press toward the sashing.

17. Sew the dark green 1½" squares and the remaining dark green triangles cut from 2⅝" squares to the ends of the remaining 1½" x 15½" medium green sashing pieces to form the sashing rows as shown. Press toward the medium green rectangles.

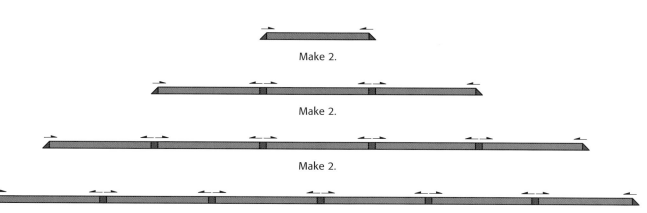

Make 2.

Make 2.

Make 2.

Make 1.

18. Sew the block rows and sashing rows together to form the quilt top. Press toward the sashing rows.

19. Sew three of the dark gold 1½"-wide strips together end to end to form one long strip for the inner border. Repeat. Measure the quilt from top to bottom and cut each strip to that measurement. Sew the strips to each side of the quilt. Press toward the inner border.

20. Sew two of the dark gold 1½"-wide strips together end to end to form one long strip. Repeat. Measure the quilt from side to side (including borders just added) and cut each strip to that measurement. Sew the strips to the top and bottom of the quilt. Press toward the inner border.

21. Measure the quilt from top to bottom and cut two of the dark green 9½"-wide strips to that measurement. Sew the strips to each side of the quilt. Press toward the outer border.

22. Measure the quilt from side to side (including borders just added) and cut the two remaining dark green 9½"-wide strips to that measurement. Sew the strips to the top and bottom of the quilt. Press toward the outer border.

23. Quilt as desired and bind.

Horizontal Ribbons

Designed by Susan Dissmore, sewn by Lorri Gellerson, and machine quilted by Eileen Peacher, 2005.

QUILT ESSENTIALS

Finished quilt: 59" x 75"

9" blocks required: 12

A limited palette of berry red, butter yellow, deep grass green, and shades of navy blue create a smaller horizontal version of "Woven Ribbons," shown on page 59.

Block-of-the-Month Option

Since this quilt uses a limited palette of only 10 fabrics, consider purchasing all the fabric you'll need for the blocks up front. Make one block each month and focus on improving your piecing skills as you sew. When the blocks are complete, purchase the fabrics for the block frames, sashings, and outer border.

MATERIALS

Yardages are based on 42"-wide fabric.

2⅜ yards of dark blue tone-on-tone for block frames, sashing, and outer border

1⅞ yards of medium blue for block frames and sashing

1½ yards of light print for blocks

⅞ yard of light blue for block frames

¾ yard of medium green for block frames

¾ yard of dark blue print for blocks

⅝ yard of dark green for block frames

½ yard of yellow floral print for blocks

½ yard of red print for blocks

¼ yard of light green print for blocks

⅝ yard of fabric for binding

4 yards of fabric for backing

67" x 83" piece of batting

CUTTING

All measurements include ¼" seam allowance. For the blocks, see the cutting directions on pages 18–29. Cut the lengthwise border pieces from the dark blue tone-on-tone after cutting all the other pieces.

From the light print, dark blue print, yellow floral, red print, and light green print, cut:

- Pieces for a total of 12 blocks

From the medium blue, cut:

- 18 strips, 1½" x 42"
- 2 strips, 15½" x 42"; from them, cut 31 rectangles, 1½" x 15½"

From the light blue, cut:

- 16 strips, 1½" x 42"

From the dark blue tone-on-tone, cut:

- 6 strips, 1½" x 42"
- 1 strip, 1½" x 42"; from it, cut 20 squares, 1½" x 1½"
- 4 strips, 5½" x length of fabric

From the dark green, cut:

- 2 strips, 7½" x 42"

From the medium green, cut:

- 2 strips, 9½" x 42"; from them, cut 48 rectangles, 1½" x 9½"

ASSEMBLY

1. Make 12 blocks, following the assembly instructions on pages 18–29. Each block should measure 9½" x 9½".

2. Sew 10 medium blue and 8 light blue 1½"-wide strips together to form two strip sets.

Press toward the light blue. Crosscut the strip sets into 48 segments, 1½" wide.

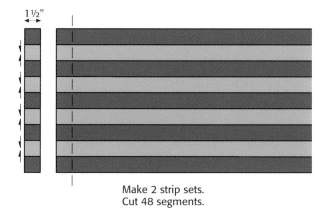

1½"

Make 2 strip sets.
Cut 48 segments.

3. Sew the dark, medium, and light blue 1½"-wide strips together into strip sets as shown. Press toward the medium blue. Make four of strip set A and crosscut 96 segments, 1½" wide. Make two of strip set B and crosscut 48 segments, 1½" wide.

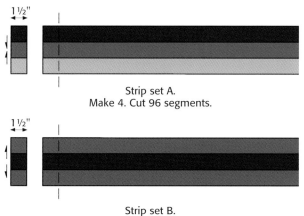

1½"

Strip set A.
Make 4. Cut 96 segments.

1½"

Strip set B.
Make 2. Cut 48 segments.

4. Sew the crosscut segments from step 3 together to form Nine Patch blocks as shown. Press.

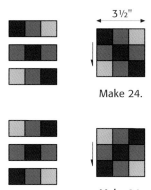

3½"

Make 24.

Make 24.

5. Sew a light blue 1½"-wide strip to each side of the dark green 7½"-wide strips. Make two strip sets. Press toward the light blue. Crosscut the strip sets into 48 segments, 1½" wide.

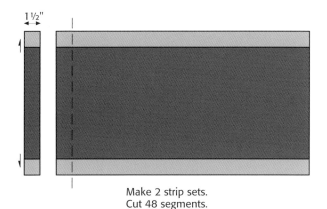

1½"

Make 2 strip sets.
Cut 48 segments.

6. Join the units from step 2, step 5, and the medium green 1½" x 9½" rectangles to form the block frames. Press toward the green rectangles.

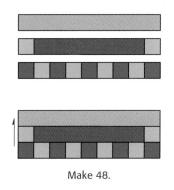

Make 48.

7. Sew the Nine Patch blocks from step 4 to each side of 24 of the units from step 6. Press.

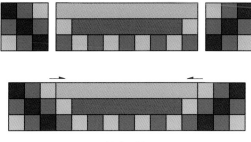

Make 24.

8. Sew the remaining units from step 6 to opposite sides of the 12 blocks from step 1. Press.

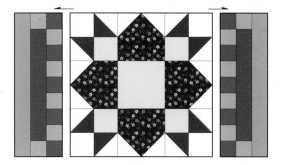

9. Sew the units from step 7 to the remaining sides of the blocks from step 8. Press.

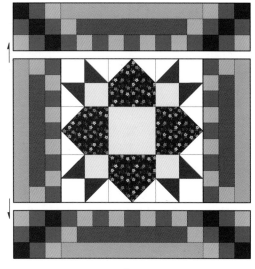

Make 12.

10. Sew four dark blue 1½" squares and three 1½" x 15½" medium blue sashing pieces together to form a sashing row as shown. Press toward the medium blue. Make 5.

Make 5.

11. Sew the blocks and the remaining medium blue 1½" x 15½" sashing pieces together into rows. Press toward the medium blue.

12. Sew the block rows and sashing rows together to form the quilt top. Press toward the sashing rows.

13. Measure the quilt from top to bottom and cut two of the dark blue 5½"-wide strips to that measurement. Sew the strips to each side of the quilt. Press toward the outer border.

14. Measure the quilt from side to side (including borders just added) and cut the two remaining dark blue 5½"-wide strips to that measurement. Sew the strips to the top and bottom of the quilt. Press toward the outer border.

15. Quilt as desired and bind.

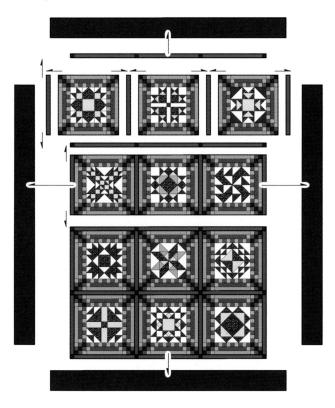

No Way Out

Designed and sewn by Susan Dissmore; machine quilted by Sue Gantt, 2005.

QUILT ESSENTIALS

Finished quilt: 63" x 81"
9" blocks required: 18

An inner border of fuchsia and a chain of black and gray close all exits to these 18 vibrant blocks colored in turquoise, purple, green, and blue.

Block-of-the-Month Option

At the start of the project, purchase 2 yards of a white-and-black print and 1 yard of a multicolored print for the 18 blocks. Select fat quarters (or fat eighths) each month for nine months to make two blocks per month. Save the scraps for later use. To complete the quilt, purchase complementary fabrics for the alternate Nine Patch and outer border blocks. (I used black, medium gray, light gray, and dark pink.)

MATERIALS

Yardages are based on 42"-wide fabric.

2⅜ yards of black print for the Nine Patch and outer border blocks

2 yards of white-and-black print for block backgrounds

1⅞ yards of light gray print for the Nine Patch and outer border blocks

1¼ yards of medium gray print for the Nine Patch blocks

1 yard of multicolored print for blocks

⅜ yard of dark pink for the outer border blocks

7 fat quarters of assorted medium purple, dark purple, turquoise, blue, and green prints for blocks

1 fat eighth *each* of medium purple, dark purple, and turquoise for blocks (3 total)

¾ yard of fabric for binding

5 yards of fabric for backing

71" x 89" piece of batting

CUTTING

All measurements include ¼" seam allowance. For the blocks, see the cutting directions on pages 18–29.

From the white-and-black print, cut:

- Pieces for a total of 18 blocks

From the multicolored print, cut:

- Pieces for a total of 18 blocks

From the 7 assorted medium and dark fat quarters, cut:

- Pieces for a total of 18 blocks

From the medium purple, dark purple, and turquoise fat eighths, cut:

- Pieces for a total of 18 blocks

From the black print, cut:

- 21 strips, 1½" x 42"
- 1 strip, 4½" x 42"; from it, cut 4 rectangles, 4½" x 5½"
- 4 strips, 4½" x 42"
- 2 strips, 9½" x 42"; from them, cut 14 rectangles, 4½" x 9½"

From the medium gray print, cut:

- 26 strips, 1½" x 42"

From the light gray print, cut:

- 11 strips, 1½" x 42"
- 6 strips, 3½" x 42"; from them, cut 82 rectangles, 2½" x 3½", and 4 rectangles, 3½" x 5½"
- 2 strips, 2½" x 42"; from them, cut 20 squares, 2½" x 2½"
- 4 strips, 3½" x 42"

From the dark pink, cut:

- 1 strip, 1½" x 42"; from it, cut 4 rectangles, 1½" x 2½". Reserve the remainder of the strip.
- 4 strips, 1½" x 42"

ASSEMBLY

1. Make two each of nine blocks, following the assembly directions on pages 18–29. Each block should measure 9½" x 9½".

2. Sew the black, medium gray, and light gray 1½"-wide strips together to form seven strip sets. Press as shown. Crosscut the strip sets into 176 segments, 1½" wide.

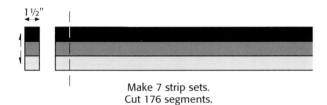

1½"

Make 7 strip sets.
Cut 176 segments.

3. Sew the black and medium gray 1½"-wide strips together into strip sets as shown. Press toward the black. Make five of strip set A and crosscut 115 segments, 1½" wide. Make two of strip set B and crosscut 44 segments, 1½" wide.

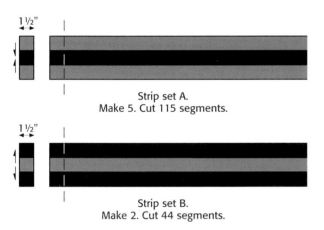

1½"

Strip set A.
Make 5. Cut 115 segments.

1½"

Strip set B.
Make 2. Cut 44 segments.

4. Sew the crosscut segments from steps 2 and 3 together to form the Nine Patch blocks and partial Nine Patch blocks as shown. Press.

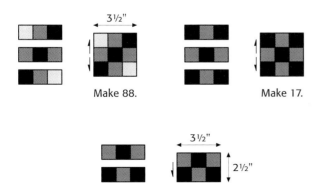

3½"

Make 88.   Make 17.

3½"

2½"

Make 10.

5. Sew six medium gray and three light gray 1½"-wide strips together into three strip sets. Press toward the light gray and crosscut the strip sets into 78 segments, 1½" wide.

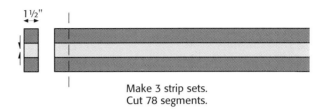

1½"

Make 3 strip sets.
Cut 78 segments.

6. Sew the segments from step 5 to the light gray 2½" x 3½" rectangles. Press toward the rectangles. Each unit should measure 3½" x 3½".

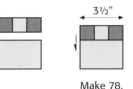

3½"

Make 78.

7. Sew the remaining light gray and medium gray 1½"-wide strips together into one strip set. Press toward the light gray and crosscut the strip set into 20 segments, 1½" wide.

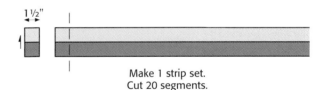

1½"

Make 1 strip set.
Cut 20 segments.

8. Sew the units from step 7 to the light gray 2½" squares. Press toward the light gray squares.

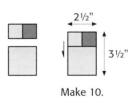

2½"

3½"

Make 10.

Make 10.

9. Sew the Nine Patch blocks from step 4 and the units from step 6 together into rows. Press as shown. Sew the rows together to form the Double Nine Patch block. Press. Each block should measure 9½" x 9½".

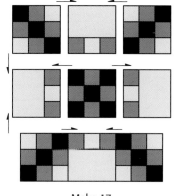

Make 17.

10. Sew the remaining units from steps 4, 6, and 8 into rows. Press as shown. Sew the rows together to form a rectangle unit that measures 5½" x 9½". Press.

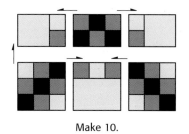

Make 10.

11. Sew the black 4½" x 9½" rectangles to the top of the units from step 10. Press toward the black rectangles. Each block should measure 9½" x 9½".

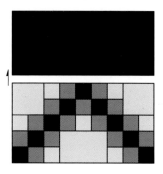

Make 10.

12. Sew the 4½"-wide black strips, 3½"-wide light gray strips, and 1½"-wide dark pink and black strips together into four strip sets. Press as shown. Crosscut the strip sets into 14 blocks, 9½" x 9½".

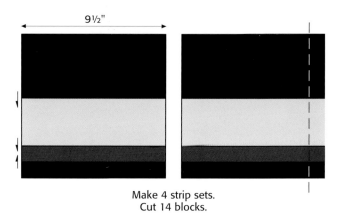

9½"

Make 4 strip sets.
Cut 14 blocks.

13. Sew the remainder of the dark pink 1½"-wide strip and the black 1½"-wide strip together to form one strip set. Press toward the black and crosscut the strip set into four segments, 1½" wide.

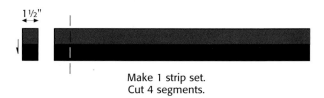

1½"

Make 1 strip set.
Cut 4 segments.

14. Sew the segments from step 13 to the dark pink 1½" x 2½" rectangles and the light gray 2½" x 3½" and 3½" x 5½" rectangles to form a square that measures 5½" x 5½". Press as shown.

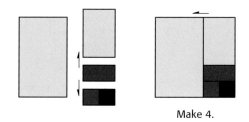

Make 4.

15. Sew the black 4½" x 5½" rectangles and 4½" x 9½" rectangles to the squares from step 14. Press toward the black rectangles. Each block should measure 9½" x 9½".

16. Sew the blocks from steps 1, 9, 11, 12, and 15 together into rows as shown in the quilt diagram. Press seams in the opposite direction from row to row.

17. Sew the rows together to form the quilt top. Press.

18. Quilt as desired and bind.

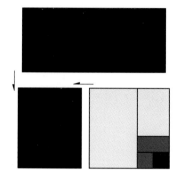

Make 4.

Lively Logs

Designed and sewn by Susan Dissmore; machine quilted by Eileen Peacher, 2004.

QUILT ESSENTIALS

Finished quilt: 67" x 85"

9" blocks required: 18

Feed sack prints and bubblegum pinks reminiscent of the 1930s give an air of nostalgia to this quilt made of 18 pieced blocks and 17 alternate Half Log Cabin blocks. Reproduction prints are often bundled in fat quarter or fat eighth cuts, which are the perfect size when you need to collect a wide variety of color and scale.

Block-of-the-Month Option
At the start of the project, purchase 2½ yards of an off-white for the block backgrounds. Select fat eighths (or fat quarters) each month for nine months to make two blocks per month. To complete the quilt, choose complementary fat quarters (or use your scraps) for the Half Log Cabin blocks. When the top is done, audition fabrics for the final outer border.

MATERIALS

Yardages are based on 42"-wide fabric.

25 fat eighths of assorted medium and dark prints for blocks

2¾ yards of blue stripe for outer border (2½ yards for nonmitered corners)

2½ yards of off-white for blocks and inner border★

10 fat quarters★★ of assorted dark prints for Half Log Cabin blocks

6 fat quarters★★ of assorted light prints for Half Log Cabin blocks

¾ yard of fabric for binding

5¼ yards of fabric for backing

75" x 93" piece of batting

★ ½ yard is allowed for the inner border.

★★ Scraps may be used as a substitute for the fat quarters.

CUTTING

All measurements include ¼" seam allowance. For the blocks, see the cutting directions on pages 18–29.

From the off-white, cut:
- Pieces for a total of 18 blocks
- 8 strips, 2" x 42"

From the assorted medium and dark print fat eighths, cut:
- Pieces for a total of 18 blocks

From *each* of the 10 assorted dark print fat quarters, cut:
- 10 strips, 1⅝" x 21" (100 total)

From *each* of the 6 assorted light print fat quarters, cut:
- 10 strips, 1⅝" x 21" (60 total)

From the blue stripe, cut:
- 4 strips, 5½" x length of fabric

ASSEMBLY

1. Make two each of nine blocks, following the assembly directions on pages 18–29. Each block should measure 9½" x 9½".

2. Sew 10 light print 1⅝"-wide strips and 10 dark print 1⅝"-wide strips into pairs to form strip sets. Press toward the dark fabric. Crosscut the strip sets into 120 segments, 1⅝" wide.

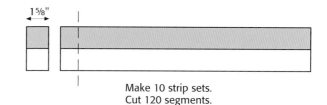

Make 10 strip sets.
Cut 120 segments.

3. With right sides together, randomly sew the units from step 2 to dark 1⅝"-wide strips as shown. Press toward the added strip and trim each unit from the strip to 2¾" x 2¾" square.

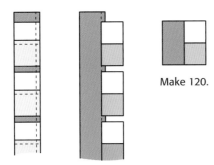

Make 120.

4. With right sides together, randomly sew the units from step 3 to the light print 1⅝"-wide strips as shown. Press toward the added strips and trim each unit from the strip to 2¾" x 3⅞".

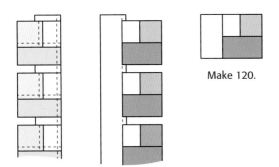

Make 120.

5. Continue adding strips and trimming as shown to form the Half Log Cabin blocks. Make 120 blocks.

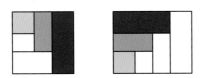

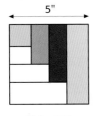

5"

Make 120.

6. Using 68 of the blocks from step 5, make 17 larger blocks that measure 9½" x 9½". Press as shown.

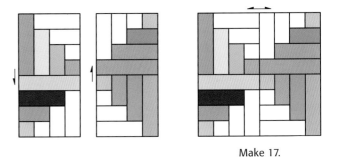

Make 17.

7. Arrange and sew the blocks from steps 1 and 6 together into rows. Press as shown. Sew the rows together to form the quilt top. Press seams open.

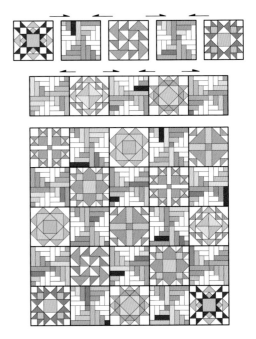

8. Sew the remaining Half Log Cabin blocks together into two rows of 12 blocks and two rows of 14 blocks as shown. Press in the opposite direction of the quilt top.

Make 2.

Make 2.

9. Sew the longer rows from step 8 to the sides of the quilt top. Press. Sew the remaining shorter rows to the top and bottom of the quilt. Press.

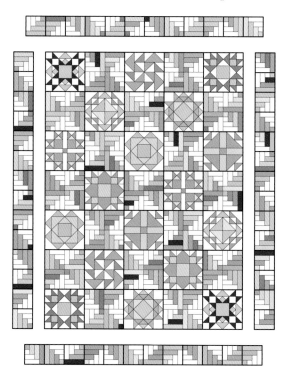

10. Sew two of the off-white inner-border strips together end to end to form one long strip. Repeat to make four strips. Press.

11. Measure the quilt top from top to bottom and cut two of the off-white strips to that measurement. Sew the strips to the sides of the quilt. Press toward the border.

12. Measure the quilt top from side to side (including borders just added) and cut the remaining two off-white strips to that measurement. Sew the strips to the top and bottom of the quilt. Press toward the border.

13. Measure the quilt top from top to bottom and side to side. Add a total of 16" to each of the measurements and cut the blue stripe strips to those lengths. (For the mitered corners, you need 8" extra on each end of the border strip.) Starting ¼" from the corner of the quilt, sew a longer strip to each side of the quilt, leaving the 8" tail on each end free. Sew the shorter top and bottom strips to the quilt in the same manner.

14. With right sides together, fold the quilt top in half diagonally, matching up the border strips. Place a ruler along the folded edge of the quilt, lining up the 45° line along the raw edge of the border strip, and draw a diagonal line. Pin and sew the strips together on the drawn line. Cut away the excess fabric and press the seams open.

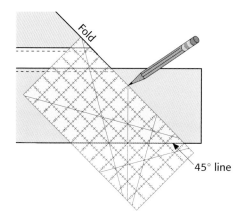

15. Quilt as desired and bind.

TREASURED TIP

Because I used a blue stripe for the border, I chose to miter the corners. If you don't use a stripe, mitering is not necessary.

Asian Elegance

Designed and sewn by Susan Dissmore; machine quilted by Eileen Peacher, 2004.

QUILT ESSENTIALS

Finished quilt: 90" x 90"

9" blocks required: 17

Block frame: Pandora's Box

A zigzag border of a deep blue and a light print frames the subtle shading of vibrant reds and lush greens that accent the captivating crane print in this magnificently composed quilt. Although only 12 fabrics were used in this quilt, lots of additional fabrics could be selected for the blocks and borders to make it scrappier.

Block-of-the-Month Option

Purchase the crane print (or main print of your choice) and the light print when you begin the project. Then choose other fabrics each month to contrast and coordinate with the colors found in the main print. Make two blocks each month before adding borders and assembling the quilt.

MATERIALS

Yardages are based on 42"-wide fabric.

3½ yards of light print for blocks and zigzag borders

2⅝ yards of crane print for setting triangles and shaded squares border

2¼ yards of dark blue print for blocks and zigzag border

1½ yards of dark green print for blocks, block frame, and inner border

1 yard of dark red print for blocks and shaded square border

1 yard of medium red print for blocks, block frame, and shaded square border

1 yard of dark blue-and-red floral print for blocks and accent strips

1 yard of red-and-green floral print for blocks, block frame, and shaded square border

⅞ yard of multicolored fan print for blocks and shaded square border

¾ yard of medium green print for blocks and shaded square border

¼ yard of light blue print for blocks

¼ yard of gold print for blocks

⅞ yard of fabric for binding

8¼ yards of fabric for backing

98" x 98" piece of batting

CUTTING

All measurements include ¼" seam allowance. For the blocks, see the cutting directions on pages 18–29. For the Pandora's Box block frame, see page 30.

From all fabrics for the blocks, cut:

- Pieces for a total of 17 blocks

From the light print, cut:

- 4 strips, 7¼" x 42"; from them, cut 17 squares, 7¼" x 7¼". Cut the squares diagonally twice to yield 68 triangles.
- 9 strips, 3⅞" x 42"; from them, cut 84 squares, 3⅞" x 3⅞". Cut the squares diagonally once to yield 168 triangles.

From the dark blue print, cut:

- 4 strips, 7¼" x 42"; from them, cut 17 squares, 7¼" x 7¼". Cut the squares diagonally twice to yield 68 triangles.
- 9 strips, 3⅞" x 42"; from them, cut 84 squares, 3⅞" x 3⅞". Cut the squares diagonally once to yield 168 triangles.

From the crane print, cut:

- 1 strip, 12⅞" x 42"; from it, cut 2 squares, 12⅞" x 12⅞". Cut the squares diagonally once to yield 4 triangles.
- 3 strips, 14" x 42"; from them, cut 6 squares, 14" x 14". Cut the squares diagonally twice to yield 24 triangles.
- 2 strips, 7¼" x 42"; from them, cut 8 squares, 7¼" x 7¼". Cut the squares diagonally once to make 16 triangles.
- 7 strips, 2" x 42"

From the dark green print, cut:

- Pieces for 1 block frame (patches E, F)
- 7 strips, 2¼" x 42"
- 4 rectangles, 2" x 2¼"
- 8 strips, 1⅜" x 42"

From the dark red print, cut:

- 7 strips, 2¼" x 42"

From the medium red print, cut:

- Pieces for 1 block frame (patches A, B)
- 7 strips, 2" x 42"

From the dark blue-and-red floral print, cut:

- 2 strips, 1½" x 42"; cut the strips into 2 rectangles, 1½" x 15½", and 2 rectangles, 1½" x 17½"
- 4 strips, 1⅜" x 42"; cut the strips into 2 rectangles, 1⅜" x 36½", and 2 rectangles, 1⅜" x 38¾"

From the red-and-green floral print, cut

- Pieces for 1 Pandora's Box frame (patches C, D)
- 7 strips, 2" x 42"

From the multicolored fan print, cut

- 7 strips, 2" x 42"

From the medium green print, cut:

- 7 strips, 2" x 42"

ASSEMBLY

1. Make 17 blocks, following the assembly directions on pages 18–29. I made one Corn and Beans block and four each of the Christmas Star, Crown of Thorns, Snowflakes, and Honeymoon blocks. Each block should measure 9½" x 9½".

2. Make one Pandora's Box block frame using the dark green print, medium red print, and red-and-green floral print pieces and following the assembly directions on page 31. Sew the frame to your chosen center block. The framed block should measure 15½" x 15½".

3. Sew the 1½" x 15½" dark blue-and-red print strips to the top and bottom of the block from step 2. Press toward the strips. Sew the 1½" x 17½" dark blue-and-red print strips to each side. Press toward the strips.

Make 1.

4. Sew the crane print triangles cut from 12⅞" squares to each side of the block from step 3. Press toward the triangles and trim the dog-ears. The block should measure 24½" x 24½".

5. Sew the light print and dark blue triangles cut from 3⅞" squares together along the longest

edge. Press toward the dark blue and trim the dog-ears.

Make 32.

6. Arrange and sew the half-square-triangle units from step 5 into rows. Sew the rows together to form the corner blocks of the zigzag border. Press as shown.

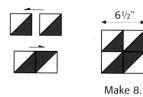

6½"

Make 8.

7. Sew the light print triangles cut from 3⅞" squares to each side of the dark blue triangles cut from 7¼" squares. Press toward the light print triangles.

Make 68.

8. Sew the dark blue triangles cut from 3⅞" squares to each side of the light print triangles cut from 7¼" squares. Press toward the blue triangles.

Make 68.

9. Sew the units from steps 7 and 8 together to form the zigzag border blocks. Press half of the blocks in one direction and the other half in the opposite direction.

6½"

Make 34 of each.

10. Sew four of the blocks from step 9 together to form a row. Repeat to make four rows. Press seams open.

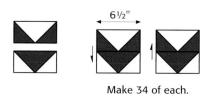

Make 4.

11. Sew a row from step 10 to each side of the center section as shown. Press toward the center section. Sew a zigzag corner block from step 6 to each side of the two remaining border rows and sew them to the top and bottom of the center section. Press. Reserve the remaining blocks from steps 6 and 9 for the outer border.

12. Sew the 1⅝" x 36½" dark blue-and-red floral print strips to the top and bottom of the center section from step 11. Press toward the strips. Sew the 1⅝" x 38¾" dark blue-and-red floral print strips to each side. Press toward the strips.

13. Sew the crane print triangles cut from 14" squares to the sides of the remaining blocks from step 1 to make rows as shown. Press toward the triangles. Sew the crane print triangles cut from 7¼" squares to each end. Press seams open.

Make 2.

Make 2.

14. Sew the two shorter rows to the top and bottom of the quilt. Press toward the added border. Sew the two larger rows to the sides of the quilt. Press toward the border just added.

15. Sew the 2"- and 2¼"-wide strips cut from the various fabrics for the shaded square border into seven strip sets of seven strips each as shown. The 2¼" dark green and dark red strips should be placed on the outside edges. Press each seam in the opposite direction of the previous seam. Crosscut the strip sets into 140 segments, 2" wide.

Make 7 strip sets.
Cut 140 segments.

16. Sew 30 of the segments from step 15 together to make a row as shown. Repeat to make four shaded border strips. Press the seams in one direction.

Make 4.

17. Trim each border row to 6¾" wide, leaving a ¼" seam allowance along the edges as shown.

Trim.

Trim.

18. Remove portions of five remaining border segments as shown. Sew the segments together in the same manner as described in step 16, adding the dark green 2" x 2¼" rectangles to one end as shown. Repeat to make four corner triangle units. Press in one direction and trim the edges, leaving a ¼" seam allowance as shown in step 17.

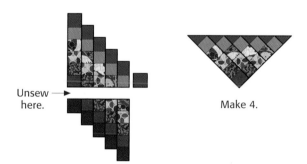

Unsew here.

Make 4.

19. Sew the corner triangle units from step 18 to the right-hand side of each of the shaded square border rows from step 17 as shown.

20. Sew the border rows from step 19 to each side of the quilt top, starting and stopping ¼" from the edges. Press the seam toward the center of the quilt. Align the unstitched corners and pin them together. Sew the seams, beginning at the inside corner and stitching toward the outside corner, removing pins as you come to them. Press the seams open.

Sew the 1⅜" x 42" dark green print strips together end to end in pairs to make four long strips. Cut two pieced strips to 76¾" long. Sew these strips to the top and bottom of the quilt. Press toward the dark green strips.

22. Cut the remaining pieced strips to 78½" long. Add these strips to the sides of the quilt. Press toward the dark green strips.

23. Sew 13 of the remaining zigzag blocks from step 9 together in the same manner as described in step 10. Repeat to make four border rows. Sew the remaining corner blocks from step 6 to each side of two border rows. Sew the borders to the quilt as shown. Press.

24. Quilt as desired and bind.

AUTUMN SPLENDOR TABLE RUNNER

13" x 51".
Designed by Susan Dissmore; sewn and machine quilted by Kitty Bailey, 2004.

Stitch three or four blocks and simply add setting triangles using your favorite print to create a quick-and-easy table runner. (See step 13 of "Asian Elegance" on page 82.)

Quilts Using Orphan Blocks

Floral Elegance Table Topper

Designed by Susan Dissmore; sewn and machine quilted by Kitty Bailey, 2004.

QUILT ESSENTIALS

Finished quilt: 36" x 36"

9" blocks required: 1

Block frame: Pandora's Box

Using a lightly colored rose floral print and a zigzag border, you can quickly turn one framed block into a table topper or wall hanging.

MATERIALS

Yardages are based on 42"-wide fabric.

⅞ yard of light beige floral for Weathervane block and zigzag border

⅞ yard of green tone-on-tone for block frame and zigzag border

½ yard of large-scale floral print for setting triangles

⅜ yard of dark pink for Weathervane block and block frame

⅜ yard of blue floral print for Weathervane block and block frame

¼ yard of dark blue for Weathervane block and inner border

⅜ yard of fabric for binding

1¼ yards of fabric for backing

42" x 42" piece of batting

CUTTING

All measurements include ¼" seam allowance. For the Weathervane block, see cutting directions on page 27. For the Pandora's Box block frame, see page 30.

From the light beige floral, cut:

- Pieces for 1 Weathervane block (patches A, B)
- 1 strip, 7¼" x 42"; from it, cut 4 squares, 7¼" x 7¼". Cut the squares diagonally twice to yield 16 triangles.
- 3 strips, 3⅞" x 42"; from them, cut 24 squares, 3⅞" x 3⅞". Cut the squares diagonally once to yield 48 triangles.

From the dark pink, cut:

- Pieces for 1 Weathervane block (patches C, D)
- Pieces for 1 Pandora's Box block frame (patches A, B)

From the blue floral print, cut:

- Pieces for 1 Weathervane block (patch E)
- Pieces for 1 Pandora's Box block frame (patch C, D)

From the dark blue, cut:

- Pieces for 1 Weathervane block (patch F)
- 2 strips, 1½" x 42"; cut the strips into 2 rectangles, 1½" x 15½", and 2 rectangles, 1½" x 17½"

From the green tone-on-tone, cut:

- Pieces for 1 Pandora's Box block frame (patches E, F)
- 1 strip, 7¼" x 42"; from it, cut 4 squares, 7¼" x 7¼". Cut the squares diagonally twice to yield 16 triangles.
- 3 strips, 3⅞" x 42"; from them, cut 24 squares, 3⅞" x 3⅞". Cut the squares diagonally once to yield 48 triangles.

From the large-scale floral print, cut:

- 1 strip, 12⅞" x 42"; from it, cut 2 squares, 12⅞" x 12⅞". Cut the squares diagonally once to yield 4 triangles.

ASSEMBLY

1. Make one Weathervane block, following the assembly directions on page 27. The block should measure 9½" x 9½".

2. Make one Pandora's Box frame, following the assembly directions on page 31. Sew the frame to the block from step 1. The framed block should measure 15½" x 15½".

3. Sew the 1½" x 15½" dark blue strips to the top and bottom of the block from step 2. Press toward the strips. Sew the 1½" x 17½" dark blue strips to each side. Press toward the strips.

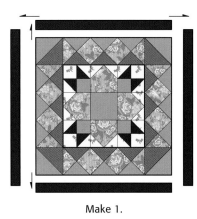

Make 1.

4. Sew the large-scale floral print triangles cut from 12⅞" squares to each side of the block from step 3. Press toward the triangles and trim the dog-ears. The block should measure 24½" x 24½".

5. Sew the light beige floral and green tone-on-tone triangles cut from 3⅞" squares together along the longest edge. Press toward the green triangles and trim the dog-ears.

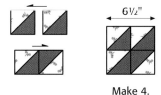

Make 16.

6. Arrange and sew the half-square-triangle units from step 5 into rows. Sew the rows together to form the corner blocks of the zigzag border. Press as shown.

Make 4.

7. Sew the light beige floral triangles cut from 3⅞" squares to each side of the green tone-on-tone triangles cut from 7¼" squares. Press toward the beige triangles.

Make 16.

8. Sew the green tone-on-tone triangles cut from 3⅞" squares to each side of the light beige floral triangles cut from 7¼" squares. Press toward the green triangles.

Make 16.

9. Sew the units from steps 7 and 8 together to form the zigzag border blocks. Press half of the blocks in one direction and the other half in the opposite direction.

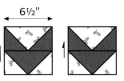

Make 8 of each.

10. Sew four of the blocks from step 9 together to form a row. Repeat to make four border rows. Press seams open.

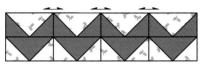

Make 4.

11. Sew two of the border rows from step 10 to each side of the unit from step 4. Press toward the center section.

12. Sew the zigzag corner blocks from step 6 to each side of the two remaining border rows from step 10. Press toward the corner blocks and sew them to the top and bottom of the unit from step 11. Press.

13. Quilt as desired and bind.

Orphan Annie

Designed, sewn, and quilted by Susan Dissmore, 2005.

QUILT ESSENTIALS

Finished quilt: 23½" x 23½"

9" blocks required: 1

Block frame: Orphan Annie

Practice your piecing skills by making the Orphan Annie frame for one block. Add an outer border to stitch this smaller version of "Perennial Patchwork," shown on page 42.

MATERIALS

Yardages are based on 42"-wide fabric.

⅝ yard of dark purple for Honeymoon block, block frame, and borders

⅜ yard of multicolored print for Honeymoon block, block frame, and border

⅜ yard of dark green for block frame and borders

¼ yard of beige for Honeymoon block and block frame

¼ yard of rust for Honeymoon block and block frame

¼ yard of rust-and-gold print for Honeymoon block

⅜ yard of fabric for binding

⅞ yard of fabric for backing

30" x 30" batting

CUTTING

All measurements include ¼" seam allowance. For the Honeymoon block, see cutting directions on page 25. For the Orphan Annie block frame, see page 34.

From the beige, cut:

- Pieces for 1 Honeymoon block (patches A, B, C)
- Pieces for 1 Orphan Annie block frame (patches A, B, C)

From the rust-and-gold print, cut:

- Pieces for 1 Honeymoon block (patch F)

From the multicolored print, cut:

- Pieces for 1 Honeymoon block (patches D, E)
- Pieces for 1 Orphan Annie block frame (patch D)
- 2 strips, 2⅛" x 42"; from them, cut 32 squares, 2⅛" x 2⅛"

From the rust, cut:

- Pieces for 1 Honeymoon block (patch G)
- Pieces for 1 Orphan Annie block frame (patches E, F)

From the dark purple, cut:

- Pieces for 1 Honeymoon block (patch H)
- Pieces for 1 Orphan Annie block frame (patches G, H)
- 1 strip, 3½" x 42"; from it, cut 7 squares, 3½" x 3½". Cut the squares diagonally twice to yield 28 triangles.
- 1 strip, 2⅛" x 42"; from it, cut 6 squares, 2⅛" x 2⅛". Cut the squares diagonally once to make 12 triangles.
- 4 strips, 1¾" x 42"

From the dark green, cut:

- Pieces for 1 Orphan Annie block frame (patches I, J)
- 1 strip, 3½" x 42"; from it, cut 7 squares, 3½" x 3½". Cut the squares diagonally twice to yield 28 triangles.
- 2 squares, 2⅛" x 2⅛"; cut the squares diagonally once to make 4 triangles
- 2 strips, 1¾" x 42"; from them, cut 2 strips, 1¾" x 14¼", and 2 strips, 1¾" x 16¾"

Assembly

1. Make one Honeymoon block, following the assembly directions on page 25. The block should measure 9½" x 9½".

2. Make one Orphan Annie block frame, following the assembly directions beginning on page 35. Sew the frame to the block from step 1. The framed block should measure 14¼" x 14¼".

3. Sew the dark green 1¾" x 14¼" rectangles to the sides of the framed block from step 2. Press toward the dark green. Sew the dark green 1¾" x 16¾" rectangles to the top and bottom of the block. Press toward the dark green.

4. Sew 24 each of the dark green and dark purple triangles cut from 3½" squares to opposite sides of the multicolored print squares. Press toward the triangles.

Make 24.

5. Sew the remaining dark green and dark purple triangles cut from 3½" squares to one side of the remaining multicolored print squares. Press toward the triangles.

Make 4.   Make 4.

6. Sew seven units from step 4 and two units from step 5 together to form a row. Add the dark purple triangles cut from 2⅛" squares to each end to form the outer-border units as shown. Repeat to make two rows. Press in one direction.

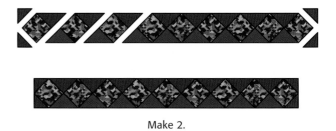

Make 2.

7. Sew five units from step 4 and two units from step 5 together to form a row. Add the dark purple and green triangles cut from 2⅛" squares to each end to form the outer border units as shown. Repeat to make two rows. Press in one direction.

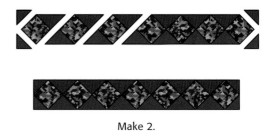

Make 2.

8. Sew the shorter border units from step 7 to the sides of the quilt. Press toward the dark green strips. Sew the longer border units from step 6 to the top and bottom of the quilt. Press toward the dark green strips.

Alternate colorway for "Orphan Annie"

9. Measure the quilt from top to bottom and cut two dark purple 1¾"-wide strips to that measurement. Sew the strips to each side of the quilt. Press toward the dark purple strips.

10. Measure the quilt from side to side (including borders just added) and cut the remaining dark purple 1¾"-wide strips to that measurement. Sew the strips to the top and bottom of the quilt. Press toward the dark purple strips.

11. Quilt as desired and bind.

Resources

For additional 9" block options, consider the following books:

Hopkins, Judy. *Around the Block with Judy Hopkins.* Woodinville, WA: That Patchwork Place, 1994.

Hopkins, Judy. *Around the Block Again.* Woodinville, WA: Martingale & Company, 2000.

Hopkins, Judy. *Once More Around the Block.* Woodinville, WA: That Patchwork Place, 2003.

McCloskey, Marsha. *Marsha McCloskey's Block Party.* Emmaus, PA: Rodale, Inc., 1998.

Bibliography

In addition to *Once More Around the Block* by Judy Hopkins and *Marsha McCloskey's Block Party* by Marsha McCloskey, both already listed in "Resources," I found the following publications to be quite helpful as I was writing this book:

Brackman, Barbara. *Encyclopedia of Pieced Quilt Patterns.* Paducah, KY: American Quilter's Society, 1993.

Malone, Maggie. *5,500 Quilt Block Designs.* New York: Sterling Publishing Co., Inc., 2003.

About the Author

Susan Teegarden Dissmore began quilting in 1994 after opening her fabric shop. About two years later, she began designing her own quilts for exclusive use at the shop. She enjoys the design process and loves to incorporate scraps into most of her quilt projects. Susan was born and raised in eastern Washington. She is a nonpracticing Certified Public Accountant. She and her husband, Tim, have two sons, Blake and Justin. Susan and her family reside in Federal Way, Washington.

www.suesrags.com
suesrags@aol.com

New and Bestselling Titles from

Martingale® & COMPANY

America's Best-Loved Craft & Hobby Books®
America's Best-Loved Knitting Books®

That Patchwork Place®

America's Best-Loved Quilt Books®

APPLIQUÉ
Adoration Quilts
Appliqué at Play *NEW!*
Appliqué Takes Wing
Easy Appliqué Samplers
Favorite Quilts
      from Anka's Treasures *NEW!*
Garden Party
Mimi Dietrich's Baltimore Basics *NEW!*
Raise the Roof
Stitch and Split Appliqué
Tea in the Garden

FOCUS ON WOOL
Hooked on Wool
Purely Primitive
Simply Primitive
Warm Up to Wool

GENERAL QUILTMAKING
All Buttoned Up *NEW!*
Alphabet Soup
American Doll Quilts
Calendar Kids *NEW!*
Cottage-Style Quilts
Creating Your Perfect Quilting Space
Creative Quilt Collection Volume One
Dazzling Quilts *NEW!*
Follow the Dots . . . to Dazzling Quilts
Follow-the-Line Quilting Designs
Follow-the-Line Quilting Designs
      Volume Two
Fresh Look at Seasonal Quilts, A *NEW!*
Merry Christmas Quilts
Prairie Children and Their Quilts *NEW!*
Primitive Gatherings
Quilt Revival
Sensational Sashiko
Simple Traditions

LEARNING TO QUILT
Blessed Home Quilt, The
Happy Endings, Revised Edition
Let's Quilt!
Magic of Quiltmaking, The
Quilter's Quick Reference Guide, The
Your First Quilt Book (or it should be!)

PAPER PIECING
40 Bright and Bold Paper-Pieced Blocks
300 Paper-Pieced Quilt Blocks
Easy Machine Paper Piecing
Quilt Block Bonanza
Quilter's Ark, A
Show Me How to Paper Piece
Spellbinding Quilts *NEW!*

PIECING
40 Fabulous Quick-Cut Quilts
101 Fabulous Rotary-Cut Quilts
365 Quilt Blocks a Year: Perpetual Calendar
1000 Great Quilt Blocks
Better by the Dozen
Big 'n Easy
Border Workbook, 10th Anniversary
      Edition, The *NEW!*
Clever Quarters, Too *NEW!*
Lickety-Split Quilts
New Cuts for New Quilts *NEW!*
Over Easy
Sew One and You're Done
Simple Chenille Quilts
Snowball Quilts *NEW!*
Stack a New Deck
Sudoku Quilts *NEW!*
Two-Block Theme Quilts
Twosey-Foursey Quilts *NEW!*
Variations on a Theme
Wheel of Mystery Quilts

QUILTS FOR BABIES & CHILDREN
Even More Quilts for Baby
More Quilts for Baby
Quilts for Baby
Sweet and Simple Baby Quilts

SCRAP QUILTS
More Nickel Quilts
Nickel Quilts
Save the Scraps
Scraps of Time
Simple Strategies for Scrap Quilts *NEW!*
Successful Scrap Quilts from
      Simple Rectangles
Treasury of Scrap Quilts, A

CRAFTS
Bag Boutique
Greeting Cards Using Digital Photos
It's a Wrap
Miniature Punchneedle Embroidery
Passion for Punchneedle, A *NEW!*
Scrapbooking Off the Page...and on
      the Wall

KNITTING & CROCHET
365 Knitting Stitches a Year:
      Perpetual Calendar
Crochet from the Heart
Cute Crochet for Kids *NEW!*
First Crochet
First Knits
Fun and Funky Crochet
Funky Chunky Knitted Accessories
Handknit Style II *NEW!*
Knits from the Heart
Knits, Knots, Buttons, and Bows
Knitter's Book of Finishing Techniques, The
Little Box of Crocheted Hats and Scarves,
      The
Little Box of Knitted Throws, The
Little Box of Scarves, The
Modern Classics *NEW!*
Pursenalities
Saturday Sweaters
Sensational Knitted Socks
Silk Knits *NEW!*
Yarn Stash Workbook, The

Our books are available at
bookstores and your favorite
craft, fabric, and yarn retailers.
If you don't see the title
you're looking for, visit us at
www.martingale-pub.com
or contact us at:
1-800-426-3126

International: 1-425-483-3313
Fax: 1-425-486-7596
Email: info@martingale-pub.com

10/06